HE DIDN'T DIE EASY

HE DIDN'T DIE EASY

*The Search for Hope Amid Poverty,
War, and Genocide*

MARY W. KIMANI

iUniverse, Inc.
New York Lincoln Shanghai

HE DIDN'T DIE EASY
The Search for Hope Amid Poverty, War, and Genocide

iUniverse books may be ordered through booksellers or by contacting:

iUniverse
2021 Pine Lake Road, Suite 100
Lincoln, NE 68512
www.iuniverse.com
1-800-Authors (1-800-288-4677)

ISBN-13: 978-0-595-39653-5 (pbk)
ISBN-13: 978-0-595-67735-1 (cloth)
ISBN-13: 978-0-595-84056-4 (ebk)
ISBN-10: 0-595-39653-4 (pbk)
ISBN-10: 0-595-67735-5 (cloth)
ISBN-10: 0-595-84056-6 (ebk)

Printed in the United States of America

This book is dedicated to the men and women of Rwanda, Burundi, and the Democratic Republic of Congo who, by sharing their stories with me, have helped me share our story with the world.

EDITOR'S NOTE

Mary Kimani walked a solitary thinker's path as a child. Her senses were awake and fully alive to the poverty, violence, and dysfunction around her. In her mind, she recorded the sights and sounds of her surroundings, and she later began to write them down.

As an adult, Kimani went to work in Rwanda, where she witnessed the impact of the atrocities of the Rwandan genocide on the lives of individual people she met, and she was forever changed.

Her internal dialogue deepens—as does her quest for the answers to the questions that arise from the world she lives in and the rest of humanity. She is hesitant to write fearing the cohesion will be lost in emotion. Her mind is plagued by smells and shadows that lead to isolation and fear of abandonment.

Inside Kimani, as well as in each of us, fear attempts to become an innate operator upon the human spirit. Having a loss of hope instigated by her own personal trauma and tragedy as well as that which she has witnessed; she is sometimes afraid of loving. She is afraid of the consequence of violence upon her soul and the souls of those around her. Sometimes, more often than not, she is courageous and forthright, facing her fears with the force and determination that only one forced to live certain realities could know:

...The familiar sound of wailing minds.
...I pause, listen, and weep.

We have been dying a long time,
and though the bodies no longer litter the streets—
The dying has not stopped...

…Our creativity overwhelms us,
we no longer know where our consciousness ends
and where our hatred begins.
To be conscious, is to hate.

…We die a little every day…there is little else to do.
My heart is parched—
Blistered dry.
It's been broken and sore—
Waiting for this rain
that will bring back life into my inner being…
…the drops falling hard over my face, my head, and my whole
body. I feel as if I am undergoing a very special kind of baptism…

Kimani's *He Didn't Die Easy* is an absorbing, aware, and deeply zealous piece of writing that is full of spirit, humanity, emotional force, and a haunting sorrow.

Kimani's images and impressions leave the reader haunted. Her book offers an up-close and firsthand view of the daily battle inside the hearts and minds of many people living with the realities of pain, poverty, and violence, whether in Rwanda or any other conflict-ridden or post-conflict-ridden country in Africa.

She speaks of how perpetrators of violence and their victims live together under conditions of brutal poverty, emotional turmoil, daily anxiety, and downright desperation.

Both groups are, in a sense, caught up in their own terrible realities attempting to ascertain whether or not they are capable of rebuilding the everyday trust necessary for the "normal" functioning of a community.

With the haunting proximity of a whispering bystander, her questioning pulls the reader to do the same so that we all might be called to a world of healing and understanding.

Editing this piece felt as though I was witnessing the war-torn country of Rwanda with every sense. Her images will be emblazoned in my mind forever, and I will continue to pray for peace in Rwanda and other countries. More than anything, I was careful not to interrupt the dance of her visual and profound dialogue—the penetrating rhythm of her awakening soul.

Thank you, Mary, for opening a whole new world unto me and opening my heart to the plight of the people of Rwanda, not to mention for making me aware of the pain and struggle of other Africans.

I hope many will read these words and be called to a higher understanding.
May the One God always bless your endeavors. And may others be called to your cause.
Amen.

~Christie Dennis
22 Nottingham Rd
Rockville Centre, NY 11570

AUTHOR'S NOTE:
ON TRYING TO FIND ANSWERS IN
THE MIDST OF POVERTY, WAR,
AND GENOCIDE

Growing up was not easy; there was much desolation, periods of severe want, and a general sense of abandonment. These experiences were the genesis of my writing. It is writing motivated by pain; mental pain, emotional pain, physical pain, but most of all, the numbing, overpowering, inner pain that threatens to engulf me if I don't find a way to express it or deal with it.

I have written compulsively from a very young age. The older pieces, most of which are now in the chapter "Ramblings of a Troubled Mind," were my efforts at making sense of a frightening and merciless world.

Rwanda changed the focus of my writing. Suddenly, the questions weren't just about poverty and emotional violence. Covering Rwanda, as I did over a period of six years, left me gutted. Listening to the survivors of the war and genocide, as well as the perpetrators of the terrible crimes committed during this period, forced upon me terrible questions, all starting with why and ending with no answers.

Two experiences stick out in my mind up to today. One was an interview with a young man; he had been sentenced to death for the murder of one of his neighbors after pleading guilty. His trial had taken place before Rwandan laws were amended to provide lower sentences for suspects who pleaded guilty. He was held in a prison almost sixty kilometers from his home area. His wife was too poor to fend for herself, let alone visit him in prison. She had only managed one visit since his arrest nine years before.

When I went to interview her, I discovered she was obviously pregnant; moreover, she carried a young baby on her hip that could not possibly have been fathered by the man in prison. I learned from a villager that one of her richer neighbors was taking care of her, obviously in exchange for sexual favors. This woman had probably never heard of contraceptives, even if she had, she would never have been able to negotiate their use with the man to whom she was beholden. When I asked the prisoner what he feels about his wife today, he had a wry smile. "She gave up on me," he said, "and I don't blame her."

The second experience was with a young woman. She had been gang-raped multiple times during the genocide and finally opted to become a sex slave to one of the militia men. In exchange, she received his protection rather than having to endure the repeated attacks from multiple men. By the end of the genocide, she was pregnant and, as she later discovered, HIV positive. The day I interviewed her, I also got to see her son. He spoke animatedly about growing up to be a teacher.

His mother had no access to antiretrovirals. She confided he has recently had bouts of illness. He looked sickly, and she admitted that she has never told him about the rape or her HIV status, neither had she ever had him tested. She didn't want to find out, and she often struggles with negative feelings toward him. "I wish I could give him away," she told me.

I have really struggled with the stories I heard. I struggle with many issues. How could we let this happen? How can we help these people? How can we help ourselves? Where is hope? Where is healing? Where is justice? The poems and reflections in this book are about that anguished struggle to find answers amid poverty, war, and genocide.

ACKNOWLEDGMENTS

I would like to thank my siblings Ngugi, Shiko, and Njeri. They of all people might understand what drives me to write. I wish also to thank Father Magnus Rau, a Benedictine monk, without whose help I might never have finished my schooling.

I would also like to thank Vid Beldavs for having faith enough in my book to encourage me to publish. Christie Dennis, for her wonderful initial editing that gave the book more clarity than I could ever have achieved. Thank you to Abdulwahab Alkebsi, for insisting I should publish, and Internews, for all the opportunities I got through working with them to hear so many people's stories.

I would like to thank those who have shared their experiences with me. Most of all, I would like to thank all those who made it possible for me to survive poverty and violence to become what I am today—a writer and a believer.

I have been so afraid.
I start to write and I panic.
Thoughts come like a torrent, threatening to overwhelm me.
So many questions,
so many images,
so many things I want to say,
shout,
cry out—
But they refuse to come out in neat and tidy order.
And so I leave it, turn the page,
start again a few months down the line,
hoping by then there will be less turmoil,
fewer shadows jumping at me from the recesses of my mind—
But they come all over again,
the ramblings of a troubled mind.

19 March 2002

I HAVE BEEN AWAKE SINCE...

The stairwell goes nowhere.
It cascades endlessly into emptiness—
Hopes lie dashed somewhere at the end of this
infinity.

The flowers bloom,
but there is no scent.
Bees do not come here.
The apparent look of life
hides the death that encroaches day after day.
There is a weeping sound in the wind:
you won't hear it,
but I do.
It is the familiar sound of wailing minds.
I pause, listen, and weep.
There is little else to do.
We have been dying a long time,
and though the bodies no longer litter the streets,
the dying has not stopped.
We die a little every day,
peering down the stairwell that goes nowhere,
reaching in vain
for the hopes that lie dashed
somewhere at the end of this infinity.

I meet many men, women, and children in the course of my work. They tell me stories that shock me, then frighten me, and then leave me confused. I wonder how we can put up with so much, yet we smile and pretend everything is OK. We hold onto hopes that we know, subconsciously at least, will never bear fruit. We hold onto identities that only engender violence, pain, corruption, and humiliation. We hold onto anything, anything at all that will make things look better or feel better—at least for some time.

The truth, though, is that we have been dying. We are dying. And we have not stopped dying.

I saw your smile today, and it left a lump in my throat—filled my stomach with cold, icy water. I saw its broken symmetry, like a piece of clay that was in the process of being molded, and the artist somehow failed to bring out the image he wanted.

I saw your pain rise to the surface despite all your efforts. A smile filled with the poignancy and pallor of a dead infant. A smile like that of a child who is trying to be brave after her doll has just been broken.

That smile—I see it a lot here. It's a smile with a ghostlike ethereal quality, as if its wearer is dying, fading away ever so slowly.

I saw your smile today, and there was a pang in my heart, as if I was watching a person fading away, halfway in this world and halfway into the next, and the transition proving to be incredibly sad.

They gather all around me,
a cloudy mass of pent-up rage,
and I can barely see their dark, menacing faces.
I scream.
I shout.
My bowels open—
It does not stop them.
My humiliation fills them with glee,
laughter greets my fear,
and the first blows fall
like searing hot knives
across my skull.
Numbed, they become nothing but shadows in
movement,
hitting me, tearing me, cutting me.
And then…
And then it is dark merciful bliss—
The pain goes.
Hours later,
awareness comes slowly,
accompanied by pain.
Emotions follow,
torrents cascading down the waterfall of my mind—
Pain,
fear,
humiliation,
hatred,
and cold.
Torn flesh and ligaments refuse to move,
so I lay still.
Weak,
hungry,
until the darkness and oblivion

come to rescue me again.
That's how they find me,
dead inside but undead.
And in the shelter,
amid many voices
high-pitched, noisy, and urgent
like the annoying buzz of mosquitoes,
the flesh recovers, ligaments heal,
but my head doesn't.
And I often long for the comfort of silence,
the reassurance of the blissful unknowing darkness:
it doesn't come.
I have been awake since…
and when I close my eyes,
I can see the blows fall.

In the dimly lit hut
where the missionary said not to go,
I visited the prophet,
and asked him to cast stones
and see what the ancestors have to say
about this evil that has come.
In the stuffy depths of the hut
where the sun is shy of shining,
he warned me of my quest.
He warned of seeking to know that which might shatter my
mind.
In answer to his spells,
the waters in the pot remained calm, but dark,
full of betrayals,
broken promises,
broken dreams,
and dead bodies,
but none of the answers which I sought.
I stared at the ancestral calabashes,
wishing they would speak,
tell me that evil can be tempered with good,
and that, in time, the memories will not be so dark.
But nothing moved, and I sat, disconsolate, defeated.
The rat tails on the roof
remind me of all the dirty things
we had become accustomed to,
like war,
rape,
and plunder.
I paid a fee to hear the prophecy.
He mumbled,
spat in the water,
made it churn with spittle.

Rest, my daughter,
that is what the ancestors say,
that is all they can tell you today.
And so I left this place
that the white missionary said not to come to,
with the words of the prophet ringing in my ears.
Rest, my daughter,
that is all the ancestors will say...
because all would solve itself,
and it will be well.
It must be well.
And I had come all this way to get
this answer.
The answer I thought
would give me the courage to wake up tomorrow,
feed my children,
and look upon the faces of those
who caused me so much injury.
Rest, my daughter,
it will solve itself.
It will be well?

Gray clouds glide by darkly tonight,
a dark, ominous moon shines from on high—
Its cream and reddish rays fall to the ground,
disturbing our peace.
This night will not so easily pass.
It will be a long and endless night,
a long and endless night in our minds.
The air around us heaves with wrongness,
someone's insane laugher resounds through the
evening,
like the echo of unruly flood water
rushing down the eroded gulleys
that form steep waterfalls in our minds.
Shadows and darkness abound
we cannot flee—

What is this our hands have crafted?
What plant is this we have put into the ground?
We send out our children to meet the ogres,
meet the devouring creatures we have nurtured
and the acts we have perpetrated
that have become their atrocious inheritance.

I have nightmares about rape. In my dreams, I replay the stories, the many versions of how it has been done—how it can be done.

I try to forget the details of the stories I have been told. But the eyes of those women never go away. The eyes haunt me, their furtive, frightened eyes. And I dream often of how they sound when they speak about it, I have dreams of their voices—voices still trying to overcome the trembling. Voices trying to hide the fear. Voices still shaky with the shock of the terrible realization that men have the capacity to invade their innermost being, to destroy and enjoy the destroying.

In my nightmares I recall voices trying to speak normally but breaking, ashamed, overwhelmed by the ravaging terror that comes from being used, torn—invaded.

The worst thing about rape
is that it robs you of the belief
that you control the innermost parts of your being.
You come out of it
violently and permanently aware
of the vulnerability of your flesh,
with the knowledge that someone has completely
invaded your body,
and you were unable to do anything to stop them.

Rape leaves a woman hurt, lost, and incredibly angry, a prisoner in a body whose vulnerability is now terribly and frighteningly clear.

Rape leaves one aghast at God and violently angry that HE made YOU vulnerable, created you with a hole that anyone could reach at will. He made you open, reachable, by anyone, at any time, anywhere.

Rape brings to fore the mind-racking unfairness of life. Because nothing one can do to a man would amount to the same type of violation and subjugation, one cannot break a man quite the way you can break a woman. Rape wounds the soul, the psyche, and breaks the complete internal working mechanisms of a woman.

Rape destroys the most human of all human things inside us—the sanctity of self. It leaves you wondering why the gods, powers, forces—or whatever you want to call them—made women so easy to desecrate. It leaves you aware of your utter powerlessness to make God, nature, nurture—or whatever it is that made us—answer for why it made humans capable of such violence and why It, He, or She does nothing to stop the rape.

She cannot afford medicine, she is very sick, dying. She has four children.

Her uterus was ruptured and later removed, a consequence of repeated gang rapes over a period of three months, her legacy from the war. I am embarrassed to be interviewing her, to be intruding into her privacy.

Recently, they released a man who killed her family members. She knows the whereabouts of the others who raped her. None of them have been brought to trial. None of them will be. If she insists, it will mean publicizing her experience. The rapists will be sent to prison for some time, and then they will soon be released. In this country of multiple and terrible crimes, it's hard to keep people in prison too long. Anyway, there is often no space.

Even if she manages to get them jailed, she will have to live next to their angry relatives, who have been known to be dangerous. And it's a community where you need every helping hand you can get. The other women don't talk, so why should she? She has to live. So she lives.

She is determined to do something about her children even though AIDS is slowly stealing her away.

She is afraid that if she stops moving, if she stops to think about what has happened, what is happening, and what it means for her children, she might just give up and die. So she doesn't. She takes what she can from those who can help, she tries to work, and she asks me if I know somewhere where she can get medicine.

And that night, alone in my house, I cry. I don't know where to find her some medicine that she can afford. Everyone I have asked tells me about a project they are putting together to help such women, but no one tells me how to get her some medicine today.

I am the totem pole that
is slowly crumbling,
and I think that all those I meet
know.
When I sleep,
faces invade my dreams,
hazy, like the silhouetted masks,
underneath the totem pole
on a ritual night.
I curse each one of them in turn,
but they don't go away.
Their voices chant louder.
They laugh,
then perform
their obscene ritual.
And in the morning,
I think that everyone knows
about my dreaming.
In the evening, he comes to me,
this seed they produced.
Dirtied,
he tries to explain how he got into a fight this time.
He too has heard the gossip,
and has seen the curious looks they give him.
His face is permanently cast into a scowl,
his ears flared as if to listen to imagined whispers.
He knows that he too,
is a reminder of a war ritual
that peace has made obscene.
And when I put him to bed
faces come to mind,
laughter and taunts,
the searing pain of each man

plunging into me,
and the hot shame of each of them
pouring his seed into me.
And I can't tell which face has seeded this child.
It is just as well,
for if I could remember,
how I would hate this child.

I stumble inside like a crumbling totem pole,
slowly falling apart,
a thing that no one respects anymore.
Everyone is ashamed to look,
ashamed to admit
the rituals that have been performed upon us.
Peace has come, war is over.
Nobody wants to hear
about the terrible things of the past.
Nobody wants to be reminded
of the terrible things they did in the name of war.
I am the reminder they cannot erase.
I am the totem pole slowly crumbling.

On a grassy patch
by the side of a dusty road,
we sat.
You moved as if to touch me,
and in your eyes I could, for a brief moment,
see the monsters that plague my dreams.
How do you want me to explain it to you?
Where do I start?
As you sat there wondering,
I thought how I would tell it,
the agony,
the humiliation,
the torn clothes, the bleeding,
collapsing in pain,
and waking up again,
to find it all continuing,
unimpeded by my pain.
And I wondered which part I could start with.
Why on a sunny day,
on a grassy patch by the side of a dusty road,
all I can see in my mind are dark houses.
All I can hear are voices of women screaming.
All I can feel is the dark tension of waiting for the
moment our tormentors must ultimately return,
and the agonies begin again.
And I want more than anything
to share this thing I have gone through with you:
I want you to feel their cutting taunts.
I want you to observe the
competitions they held
to see who would stay on top of us the longest.
I want you to know these things
so that you can understand how I feel today.

I want you to know how it felt
when the people found us,
liberated us, set us free from our monsters,
but how will you understand?
How can you understand the emptiness of being told,
"Everything will be all right"?
And do you think
that because years have passed,
I am now at ease?
Do you think
that because today you offer your undying love,
it somehow makes it all okay?
And so I stand, walk away, say nothing.
Words have stuck in my throat,
refusing to be spoken.
I walk about blind,
searching for something—
A release from the torment,
a release from my tainted body,
never finding it.
I have been looking for acceptance and belonging,
not sex.
Please don't offer me your love.

Days after it happened to her, she still couldn't walk. Her husband would not touch her, and her children became like strangers.

She gave me the interview in whispers. She would stop talking each time someone passed, self-conscious of what had happened to her.

Rape cripples your every effort to live, to smile, to believe in yourself.

In my country about 1,400 rape cases are reported every year, about three a day. That's in Kenya, a country that is at peace. In parts of Eastern Congo, one in every three women aged eight and above has been raped, often gang-raped. Some have gone through the experience several times.

In Rwanda, I have spoken to women who were held as sex slaves, raped repeatedly, mutilated by the very men who killed their entire families. Some have conceived and borne children out of these acts of hatred.

People often tell me, "You take life too seriously. Ease up. You are too sensitive." How can I not but take life seriously? How do I ignore the pain that radiates from these women? How do I block out their anger, their brokenness? These women wish they could remove their bodies in the way one can remove a dress. They want to get a new soul, a new body that has not been so grossly attacked. How can I ignore their devastation? How can I ignore mine? How can I not but take life seriously?

I have often caught myself thinking that we talk at cross purposes when we talk about love—that sometimes what I mean, what women mean, and what men are willing to offer are different and irreconcilable.

This difference becomes particularly poignant when a woman has been abused, beaten, raped, or violated in any other way.

There is an unholy impatience with their experiences and their memories. Lovers, husbands, or would-be caregivers want that part of dealing with the violent memories done with—and fast.

And after several attempts to explain that such a thing is not possible, most women give in, pretend, and shunt the memories to a deep, dark place. Their lovers, friends, and family are now comfortable, but the women face that dark place daily. It never goes away.

The price they pay is unbearably high. It is a price that society extorts from you. You come to understand the unspoken blackmail—that if you want ever to have the comfort of the other, you must pretend it is okay.

For no man will hold you, love you, if he has also to hold and love the demons that plague your mind and heart daily. At the least, he will do it for only so long, and then he will expect you to forget. He will especially expect you to forget when engaged in lovemaking. All the while your mind is plagued with images, fears, panic, and the certain knowledge from experience that this man has the physical power, if nothing else, to force you to place you where you have been before and do not want to go again. Of course, maybe the lover, husband, and caregiver would never think of such a thing—maybe they would never do such a thing.

But the woman thinks it, feels it, and fears it all the same.

And I know many a woman who is lying underneath the burden of this heavy body on top of her, who is offering his love. She might not be seeing it as love; she might be holding her breath in terror, pretending but unable to enjoy this so-called sharing; she might be wondering when it will end so he can drop off and hold her. For it is the holding she looks forward to, the talking about irrelevancies, the gentleness of his touch when the sex thing has been done with and disposed of.

And if it was possible to have those extra things—the holding, the warm body next to her, the person to speak to—and not this sex, what paradise it would be! But no, there is no such hope.

So he keeps offering "love," and she keeps accepting what he has to offer, hating him for not knowing how she suffers, hating herself for needing someone and not wanting to be lonely, hating the world for the memories.

But what else is out there, which man out there will be willing to merely hold, hug, talk, share a bed, and not demand his pound of flesh?

I don't hate you,
I just hate life.
Sometimes,
I hate the things it can do to you.
the marks it can leave on you
the things it can take away.

I don't hate you.
I just hate the fact that
there are things I cannot rub away,
undo,
change.
You walked away from me today,
not even a backward glance.
And I understand.
It is not easy to share the same space with
these hard things,
these unclear things, these uncertain things.
If I could, I would force you to turn and stay.
I keep hoping that I will hear from you,
saying it was all a big mistake,
that we can pick up from where we left off.
I want so much to believe in us,
but I cannot do what you ask,
I cannot make it go away,
and so it is you who has gone.

Soiled sheets,
soiled emotions—
We grope each other in the dark of the night,
you looking for a piece of flesh,
me looking for love.
I hear your grunting noises,
as if from a faraway land.
I lay here
accepting it all,
thinking it will bring me love,
bring me what I need.

Only, it doesn't come.
Instead, I get soiled sheets,
soiled emotions,
and your dirty hands
groping my body in the dark of the night,
looking for a breast to hold in your rough hands,
plunging into me.
And I hear your grunting noises,
and I persevere,
thinking,
thinking…
you might learn to love me.

Racing ahead at breakneck speed—
I dare not stop,
lest the shadows catch up with me,
lest the memories catch up with me,
lest the pain returns,
lest the sorrow returns.
I am moving
at breakneck speed—
I dare not stop,
I dare not consider.
Who can bear that?
So I run.
I have the energy for that.

You can triumph over death, over hatred, and over the base things that drive men to victimize others.

You can survive. Yet in so doing, it is as if you begin a trip to a place of memories, or you begin endless efforts to submerge the memories. A trip to a place of pain, or a lifetime's effort to ignore it.

You don't notice it at first, but slowly, painfully, you come to the realization that you have crossed a bridge into a place separated from reality by an unbridgeable gulf. And from the other side, friends, family, and colleagues make helpful noises of support and their voices echo from across the gulf, a fading sound from a once familiar land.

You hold on in dead earnest to these sounds, these tendrils, which attach you to the world you once knew, the world in which you once lived. You try to lean on the support of those around, but the illusion that they understand dissipates when exposed to the slightest pressure of day-to-day living, and the anxiety they have over your ability to forget and move on.

In surviving, it is as if you cross a bridge to a place nobody can come to, nobody can share, and nobody can understand. Nobody can comprehend what it is to hear, smell, or see the things quite the way you do.

A survivor triumphs over adversity, only to enter a kind of purgatory, separated from the world, as they knew it, by the moment of terror, tragedy, or personal loss.

Life acquires a certain unfinished-ness. Things have changed and nothing can bring them back to where they were again.

One is forced to say a kind of goodbye to a world they knew which has been folded and taken away, and in exchange they have received a new world, with familiar faces, familiar sounds, familiar scents, but it is still not the one they knew. This new world has an otherworldliness to it, a half world.

Once you survive war or conflict you can be happy, you can live, but it is a different kind of happiness, a different laughter, informed as it is by the personal knowledge of having been lucky, having survived, having changed. You live; you savor life, knowing personally the sheer fragile nature of it, and its equally contradictory tenaciousness.

You become aware of the complexity of life, how love and hatred, life and death, fragility and tenaciousness somehow exist as part of the same event, same being, same person, whether victim or perpetrator. This is the reality of having survived war, violence, loss, and personal tragedy; it is a reality that any survivor anywhere in the world knows and shares and can understand. It is the reason they don't forget.

Memories don't die easy.
They rant and rave and kick.
They form ghosts—like wraiths—
that overwhelm my mind.
They fill my heart with gloom when it rains.
Call to my attention
the security man standing watch with his gun.
They hide behind the cobwebs of my mind
and come jumping in,
in the middle of laughter,
introducing that hateful pause.
They play scents and sounds over and over
in my mind,
bring to recollection bits of conversation
that make me stumble in the streets
murmuring to myself,
asking myself questions,
that I am unable to answer.
Memories don't die easy.
God knows I've been trying to kill them.

Fragments of images—children playing on the cover of a septic tank, the scent of flowers, fruit trees in season, snatches of conversations here and there—that's what memories are made of.

Memories never seem to come in a coherent, logical flow. You get snap-shots—children playing in the sawdust on a school field on a sunny day, trips from the river to fetch water, bundles of firewood, big bullyboys, the sensation of dry leaves crunching underneath your feet, your behind on fire after being tossed by a cow. Each snapshot is something meaningless to others, but to the person who remembers, it triggers all the feelings, emotions, and fears of a past time.

Memory never completes the picture. It poses a question, like the "fill-in-the—blank" test papers in school, or a friendly prompting: "Hey, remember this?"

That is why I wonder if we understand what we really mean when we tell peo-ple, "Forgive and forget."

We say it as if the offensive memory is sitting on a shelf somewhere in the mind or heart, and one merely needs to go there, remove the memory, and throw it away—there! Done!

We tell this to others because we cannot bear the burden of meeting a human being who is emotionally undressed. We encourage forgetting, burying, doing away with the things of yesterday: we encourage building new houses on the graves of yesterday. We fan hope even when lives have become unbearable, unlivable.

We hope and believe, even a bit desperately, that tomorrow will be better than today.

And that is why we do not want people getting stuck in what has happened to them.

We want forgetting. It allows us to greet each new day as if yesterday did not happen. For if we truly had to remember some yesterdays, how could we move on?

We don't want burdens, we don't want difficulties, we don't want to have to feel too deeply, and so we attempt to kill memories, and we encourage others to do the same; shove them aside, get a life, move on.

And those who have gone through war, hunger, poverty, and tragedy duly comply. They smile, move on, and keep up with society's demand not to burden others with too much remembering.

In truth, there is no forgetting. There is only desisting from saying what you remember. There is only a choice not to tell people that you still feel bad. The only real forgetting comes when the brain has died out, and the memories are no longer accessible. But there is no running, no fleeing. Every survivor of a war or tragedy knows this reality—you don't forget. You simply live.

Unwelcome thoughts
fill my mind.
Their acidic bite like a
rash from poison ivy or stinging nettles.
I wake up from my nightly dreams,
shivering from the nightmares.
I keep fanning empty hopes for tranquil nights—
nights filled with dreams of folly,
dreams of laughter.
I push the thoughts away by day,
pack every second with meaningless bustle,
unsuccessfully postponing the moment that I must
fall asleep.
And in my troubled slumber,
I flee from things that I can never outrun,
defend myself from attacks that never end,
and bury interminable numbers of bodies.
I wake up drained,
confused—
without the strength to face the world.
The taste of dying and bitter hopes fill my mouth,
I long for days without shadows moving in the dark,
when the menace lurking in my dreams
is blunted by easier times.

Wishing,
longing,
waiting.
Hoping,
desiring,
seeking.
Praying,
trying,
crying.
But there is nothing yet:
death is still death.
Time does not heal the pain.

They say time heals all wounds. Only, it doesn't. Time dulls the memory, it creates distance, and provides perspective. Sometimes time changes circumstances, and wounds recede, but time in itself has no antiseptic quality, no healing balm.

Some wounds fester in time, get worse—gangrenous. Some wounds kill, some wounds render people insane. Some wounds break people: turn them into shadows of their former selves. Some wounds heal, dry up, and leave tiny scars and foggy memories. Sometimes, like the link in a broken chain that is now soldered, some wounds actually make us better, firmer, stronger, and wiser. But though time may allow you to discover whether a wound can heal or not, it is itself, not a doctor, not a healer.

It is a cruel untruth that we have been told—that time heals all wounds. We are shown examples of people who have surmounted terrible things. We are supposed to understand that healing is possible; we are told we must be blocking our progress and our access to the power that can make us better. So we wait. Wait for time to pass, so that we can heal. And when we don't, we get bitter. And we are still waiting…

Healing is not a function of time, but a function of place, circumstances, and life. Whereas time heals some wounds, it turns others cancerous. And sometimes the only good thing that time does is to allow us to age and die, and that is what ends the pain.

HE DIDN'T DIE EASY...

Dance with me.
Let's dance a releasing dance.
A dance about the things we cannot say,
the pain we cannot heal,
the injuries we cannot undo.
Let's dance about our folly,
our cruelty,
and the things we wish we could erase—
wish away—
but cannot.
Dance with me.
Let's dance a dance of sorrow,
a dance of regret,
a dance of the pain we have put each other through.
Please dance with me.

They call themselves *Inyange za Maria* (The Egrets of Mary). Dressed in pink prison uniforms and white T-shirts, they dance, imitating the flowing movements of flying egrets with their hands, their feet stamping the ground for rhythm, each of them—thirty men in total—a killer, a self-confessed killer.

The first time I saw them, they were dancing to a song on unity and reconciliation; how they once sat side by side in church with the people they killed—neighbors, friends, and colleagues—before human politics changed allies into victims. They seemed so ordinary, yet greed and a belief in their tribe's inherent right to rule—and perhaps the perceived necessity to kill those who would, allegedly, take it away—had turned them into killers.

These previously pious men had indeed killed, raped, and tortured former friends, sometimes with glee, believing they were completely justified in their actions. But on this day, in prison, they repented. Hindsight brought moral dilemmas. Hindsight demanded taking responsibility for the murders. Hindsight asked, "Why?" So they had confessed to genocide, joined this choir, repenting, singing, and dancing about what had gone wrong, about their need for forgiveness, and their need to reconcile.

And watching them, listening to those words, I found it hard to believe that a people so fervently religious, so seemingly humbled and passionately contrite now, could have killed with equal and passionate zeal.

Hatred rages cold within your eyes.
I shiver and burn with shame:
I long to run away.
But where do I run?
I carry the voices of all those I have killed in my
head—
they tell me things I don't want to hear
about what I have become.
Reconciliation is a better word.
It allows me to move on,
it allows me to leave behind the scenes in my mind,
it helps me find myself again.
Your hatred I accept,
it is a penance for me,
it allows me to see myself as one who has paid his
dues,
it allows me to face my children.
I can live with them in confidence:
they can look up to me and love me,
What would they think if I did not seem to have
paid?
What would they think if the images in my mind became their reality?
Let's forget what happened and move on.
I promise tomorrow will be a better day.

I walk

on the

cemetery

of betrayed lives.

My every waking thought relives the condemnation

in their eyes, relives their look of horror when they

realized

who had

betrayed

them.

I live

with the

stench

of the

rotting

bodies

permanently at the back of my mind. I wonder,

at each point, whether it is the smell of any of them.

Life has become but bitter gall,

but I have no courage

to end it.

I betrayed them all to save

Myself,

but the life I saved has not proved worth the living.

The soul is corroded.
There will be no making it clean again—
The line has been crossed.
I grope through the dustbin of humanity's affection,
my hands dirty and blackened by the mire,
and I hate every inch of my being,
every aspect of my life.
If it were possible, I would tear off that part of my life
die a little,
not to have to face the ugliness of it all.
This demeaning existence…
I am choked with self-loathing,
repelled by myself,
as if from a shedding snakeskin.
I hate myself.
I truly hate myself.

The sun is setting on the mountains,
bringing to end a horrid day.
The skies are red,
stained by the blood of our children.
Our rivers are polluted
by bodies flowing downstream.
We have cursed our land.
The trees and earth flee our touch.
We have carved flesh from each other,
and over each hill and ravine,
we have dotted our roads with dismembered bodies.
The thousand hills hang their peaks with shame.
The moon deigns to shine upon our disgrace.
The rivers long for cleansing;
we have put our madness and hatred into them.
The earth groans under the weight of the bodies we
have put in it.
And the air all around us is
heavy with the weight of those we have yet to bury.
Let the sun set.
it is shaming that the heavenly bodies
should look down at the work of our hands.

Tempest,
a cauldron of struggles
on coals of hatred.
We have sown the wind,
reaped the whirlwind,
and are unable to contain the consequences
of our rabid creativity.
Tempest,
fires of ice.
We are unable to thaw our hatred,
though we constantly pump the fires of
reconciliation.
Our creativity overwhelms us;
we no longer know where our consciousness ends
and where our hatred begins.
To be conscious is to hate.

He smelled of fear.
And even as I saw them stop him,
I knew.
His life was over.
He shivered uncontrollably,
betraying his fear.
They laughed,
mocked,
and sent him in my direction.
His pants were wet by then,
but I had seen it all before.
Fear makes such children of us.
He looked at me,
eyes like a doe's.
Guileless,
Pleading,
weak,
helpless—
I swung my weapon,
breaking apart his skull.
He didn't die easy.
His eyes glazed with terror,
and the full horror of knowing that the thing he feared
had finally arrived.
There was no stopping me.
He vomited.
And I swung my weapon again,
this time splitting his head across the nose.
The fear was gone now.
There was only hatred.
I had seen that, too.
I wonder why they stop fearing
and turn to hatred at this point?

I swung the weapon again,
cutting his neck almost clear off the shoulders.

And finally, he was silent.

I feel hot.
Sweat on my brow,
heat of the sun,
stench of the bodies.
Death surrounds me,
engulfs me from within and without.
It is inside me.
I can smell its stench,
I remember the blood,
I remember the cries,
and the drying blood on my hands.
I see your mocking face peering at me
through the darkness of the night.
I hear your scornful laughter reverberate in my
bones.
I cannot flee your mocking form,
your laughing face.
Nor the sound that fills the night.
Yours is the sound
of the howling madman with whom I share this
prison.
And the madman,
The madman is me.

In the years that I have worked in Rwanda covering the aftermath of genocide, I have spoken to many men and women who have confessed to killing people.

It is difficult.

On one hand, I want to understand why they did it. On the other hand, should we really try to understand such madness?

Talking to these people is difficult because I often talk to people who never express genuine regret. It is difficult, because I am trying to understand why, and, yet, who can ever grasp how they justify what they did, how they explained it to themselves at that moment when they decided to kill?

Many have been released since I came here. They are released on grounds that they have confessed and accepted the crimes they committed, but most refuse to take full responsibility for what they have confessed.

And I often wonder how those who survived can bear to live with them, talk to them, coexist with them. And I wonder how these self-confessed killers can bear to live with themselves after everything they have done.

I am the living, walking dead.
My life scattered—
Buried in hundreds of graves around this place.
Graves,
tiny pieces of my life.
Father,
mother,
husband,
children,
brothers.
Then I
walk about
waiting to die
so that together we can be whole again.

In the mulch around the budding trees,
insects crawl about.
Snakes, salamanders, and frogs slithering and
jumping about everywhere.
The waters are dirty.
There are no fish in the sea.
We live small, dirty lives,
Damp,
Miserable,
cold lives,
full of crawling things that slither in the underbrush.
The nights are getting longer and darker,
the sun shines no more.
Weeds have overgrown the farms,
fungi thrives on every spot,
eating the very life of us
little by little.
Yeasts and other scavengers
have found residence in and on our skin.
It is as if the very heart of us is poisoned,
covered by a morass and accumulation of dirty fungi
and putrid, dying flesh.
The trees around us are bent by the weight of
the ugly emotions in the atmosphere:
I look at you and see my ugliness mirrored there.

The pit latrine is full.
They have thrown my life in there.
There is more than waste and maggots
down the pit
latrine.
There is my husband.
My child.
My mother.
My father.
The latrine is full.
They have thrown my life in there.

There are bodies in pit latrines in almost every remote part of this country—bodies killed and stashed in septic tanks along with bodily waste.

Some, wounded and not quite dead, lived on for hours in these pits and finally died by choking on human waste.

I have often asked myself about what level of hatred would make a human consign a dead human, let alone a living one, to a pit full of human waste. And my mind has never quite grasped what it is about us, as a species, that makes us so mentally disjointed, that we can do that by the day and then hold our newborn babies by the light of the candle in the evening. What do we see when we look into those new eyes, after having consigned an older life to such ignominy?

That men and women could kill in such a manner, and then copulate at night—isn't there some inherent madness in that?

There are bodies in latrines; not one, not two, not in a few exceptional cases, but hundreds of human bodies in latrines in every remote village of this tiny mountainous nation. I don't understand. I just don't understand.

Bodies floated down the river:
they were without heads.
Bodiless heads, decorated with machete wounds,
sank to the silt at the river's bed.
The remnants of our human creativity.
The air is foul with fear
heavy with despair.
Darkness descends on the noonday sun,
the weariness of our souls,
clouds the bright sky.
We are a group unwanted,
we have given up our ghosts.
The air is foul with our fear,
charged with our pain,
heavy with our despair.

I visited the asylum today and
watched you walk about,
laugh unhindered,
do as you please.
And for the first time,
I understood why you seemed so much happier,
healthier.
And I wished that,
like you,
I had gone slightly insane.
I wished that my mind had not attempted to bear all this—
Then I would not be expected to behave normally.
I would not have to wake up in the morning,
Smile,
get out of bed,
live.

Like you,
I could cry my heart out,
rant,
rave,
fall down, go berserk, and break everything.
I could make the pain go away—
Escape.

She walked right in the middle of the road, ambling sideways as she spoke to an audience that existed only in her mind.

She reminded me of another man, in another town, smartly dressed. He had mumbled as he walked, sometimes stopping suddenly to stare at the air. He sometimes posed questions to someone who was not there, getting agitated as he demanded from the unseen person "Where am I going to get money? What will I tell her? What will I tell her?"

I felt both awe and horror both times. Both the man and woman were still self-aware, properly dressed, still trying to live. I was meeting them at a point within a process, neither here, nor yet completely there.

I was witnessing a human mind unraveling, a human soul overwhelmed, trying to piece reality together. But the pieces were falling about by the wayside, and keeping the whole picture together was becoming more and more difficult.

And one day, reality would be like a jigsaw puzzle left unfinished; there would be gaping holes and pieces that do not fit. Madness would have finally arrived.

Escape from Freedom—I never finished reading the book. But I loved the title.

The title seemed to promise the ultimate escape—an escape from freedom, and all the responsibilities it entails, the expectations, the harsh realities.

I imagined being able to leave all my cares, worries, and concerns behind to escape into a world of nonexistence, nonthought, nonemotion, nonresponsibility. An escape from all the things it means to be human—flawed, needy, and broken.

I would love to escape from the struggle of trying; from the effort of aiming at something higher, attempting to achieve a better place, a better life, and a better sense of self.

Escape from Freedom—Erich Fromm wrote of it in the negative sense. But I think of the phrase with nothing but positive feelings.

To me an escape from freedom represents a release from all that is human, which from my vantage point is a mixture of the good and bad that is hard to deal with. I wish to let go of the bad, but good and bad are so inexorably linked that an escape from one is the same as a letting go of the other. An escape from freedom means a desire to flee from responsibility, from the effort it takes to change things.

But I don't care. There is so much pain in freedom that I still wish to escape.

Cold wind blows on my face,
dry lips begin to bleed.
I walk on,
determined to get to the river,
hoping it will not be too cold,
knowing it will not matter,
for I must have water.
The heavy wool does little to keep the
sharp sting of the wind from finding
an opening,
I walk on, rigid, upright,
defying the growing cold.
The skin is cracked:
my nose is sore.
I am cold through to my bones,
cold through and through.
How I wish for some warmth.
Thirst assails me,
I must have some water.
Then I wake up shivering,
hot and sweaty with fear.

There is now a constant debate, at least among those who even bother, as to whether one can continue to be patriotic to a land that bleeds, that is constantly at war, and dying, or whether there comes a time when one must look to one's own self-interests and go somewhere safer, better—abroad.

And I know that for many young, educated, brilliant Africans, this debate is no longer a luxury, it is truly a matter of life and death, a choice between staying in our broken countries and ending up in a jail or dead, or going abroad, to live and to try something new.

Twelve years ago, Keith B. Richburg, a Black American journalist working for the *Washington Post* was assigned to East Africa. He subsequently wrote the book *Out of America* in which he describes how he first saw the assignment as an opportunity to discover the continent, and a sort of homecoming.

Africa did not turn out to be what he expected. In Somalia, four of his colleagues were murdered in cold blood. And from the borders of Rwanda and Tanzania, he counted as the Akagera River swept a dead body into Lake Victoria every minute.

In South Africa, he witnessed Nelson Mandela become president in a country where dire poverty and great wealth still lived side by side.

In South Africa, he noted, they still counted bodies. In other places in Africa, he found the statistics of the dead harder to come by. And at the end of his African tour of service, he knew that he did not belong in this godforsaken place. He was not African; he was American, with all the implied meanings.

Keith could leave, not just for a while, but completely. He cut all ties. Can we?

The book elicited all the typical reactions. Keith wasn't giving much credit to Africa. Here, it was argued, was yet another journalist concentrating only on the carnage, the hunger, the bodies, and the gore. But Keith was right. In Africa, we rarely count bodies. I guess there are just too many of them. Life in Africa, to borrow the phrase, is often "nasty, brutish, and short."

And so I understand when people flee, go away, and start elsewhere, even if the societies they join don't want them, and the only job they can get is a dishwashing stint at a fast food restaurant.

I understand the logic. It is better to deal with the hatred you find abroad than face it at home, in poor countries with no infrastructure, no hospitals, and no forensics to discover how you died.

And every so often, I sometimes think that I too could find a way to emigrate, run away, and put a distance between myself and this Dark Continent, where the things we do to each other sometimes border on the incomprehensible.

Then I think of the inquisition, the holocaust, the genocide of the Armenians, the thousands killed and starved during the reign of Stalin and the Khmer Rouge, and the massacres of the Native Americans. Then I am reminded that hatred, bigotry, poverty, disaster, and violence are not synonymous to Africa. They are synonymous to humanity. Where do I go to flee from that?

THERE WOULD BE NO MAIL COMING...

Your mail has been late arriving.
I miss you.
I wish I could hear from you
know what is happening.
I fear.
There has been so much violence,
so much bloodshed,
and each silence
grows ominous.
Are you well?
Let me know.
I hear there was fighting:
was it bad?
Were you affected?
I wish you would send word—
Say you will write when things settle down,
say something,
anything.
Anything at all,
just don't keep quiet like this.
It is frightening,
unnerving.
Say you will write soon,
Please.

The photograph is of a post office in Manono, a once thriving town in Eastern Congo. When I visited, it was overgrown with grass and weeds, and the few people on its streets—soldiers, women, and children—stood wary of strangers.

The talk in the market, where wild leaves and wild fruits were on sale, was all about hunger, the raids, and rapes perpetrated by the militia and children dying because there was no medicine. The missionary doctors had long evacuated.

The post office was bombed out, but one could still see the outlines of the partitions that had served as mailrooms. Outside, rusted letterboxes stood open, gaping as if in shock, blown wide at the instant the bombs exploded.

There would be no mail coming.

The bed is hard,
and the sheets are torn.
The blanket is threadbare and old.
I have nothing else I call my own.
I am looking for something inside,
something to make up for the barrenness around me,
something to believe in,
something that will make me complete.
Consume me—
Take up every aspect of my existence
so that I can forget that the bed is hard,
the sheets are torn,
and the blankets smell of old urine.

Poverty smells. It smells of everything that we could be and we are not. Poverty stinks. It stinks of bodies not properly washed, cheap soap, and even cheaper perfumes. It smells of stale air in tiny rooms filled with human bodies of all ages. It smells of lost dignity, of copulation in tiny spaces—houses with no windows to let out the after scent of sexual fluid, nor partitions to protect young eyes that have seen too much, too soon, too often.

Poverty smells of bodies wasted by early and multiple pregnancies, and the desperation to make ends meet. It smells of lost aspirations, wasted and broken humanity, living in a haze of cheap drugs and cheaper alcohol. Poverty smells of decomposing waste uncollected. It smells of houses with no plumbing and open dumping areas for human waste. Poverty smells of disease, open wounds, festering conditions, and cheap, ineffective medicines.

The smell of poverty is the smell of small lives, used bodies, used minds, and wasted potential. It is the smell of intelligence trapped in windowless houses, struggling hard to escape. The dangerous smell of impending violence, of minds pushed too far, too often. The smell of sweat, effort, and the often unsuccessful struggle to get out of the human cesspool. Poverty smells of the despair you feel when you wake up to find that, after all your efforts, nothing has changed. You are still down.

They lied.
I have been to the mountaintop:
there is no promised land beyond.
There is no universal peace—
No water by the year 2020,
no end to all wars,
no end to the rape of women,
no end to the defilement of children.
They lied.
There is no pot of gold at the end of the rainbow—
No money to take the children to hospital,
no money for food,
no money to buy sanitary towels,
no money to buy a condom.
They lied.
Time does not heal all wounds—
I do not forget the faces,
I do not forget the laughter,
I do not forget the grunts
as they released their semen,
I do not forget the rape.

They lied. We do not grow wiser in time,
we do not learn from our experiences—
My neighbors still hate me,
and tomorrow,
another battle will be announced in the press.
We solve nothing.
They lied.
There is no justice in the world
at least, not in this world.
And I do not know if my heart can
withstand the wait to the next world.

There is no truth in this world,
no inherent justice:

They lied.

We have conceived,
(and carried our treasure in the womb)
one month too long.
Frantic,
we have run to the healers
to dispatch of this load,
that will not come out in its allotted time.
By the strength of herbs,
the muscles have contracted,
we have gone into labor.
pushed and heaved
for the child to arrive,
alas!
We have given birth to the wind.

We need hope to live, but hope is an expensive emotion. It means opening up yourself to the challenges of today because you believe that the effort will make things better tomorrow. Hope makes one vulnerable. Things may not work out, and if hope is extended too often and to no avail, it is eventually lost. We give up. We become bitter, cynical—wounded.

The loss of hope is a fatal wound for the spirit. Therefore, to protect ourselves, we have become adept at living with false hopes, false promises, and false expectations. We do so because, at a certain level in our minds, we know such promises will not come to pass, but we can pretend to believe in them—just in case we are pleasantly surprised.

We don't mind expending energy on such a farce. We understand that the promise is not a real one, so we do not invest, and we know there is little to lose. That is why we buy into statements like "Water for all by the year 2020."

We believe in such things because they help us not to have to think too much. After all, something is being done. We can believe and yet not believe at the same time. We can avoid falling into total despair or having to lay our real hopes on the line.

And so what if the efforts we have put into realizing such visions doesn't come to fruition? We knew they would not, but we did our best now, didn't we?

You have become a wilderness for me,
a place of pain,
a place of death,
a place of heartbreak.
I have called you heartbreak city.
Your wilderness has eaten my children.
Now I stare at the empty spaces,
eyes open, glazed, and unseeing.
And in the muddled stacks
of rambling thoughts, fears,
dreams, and wishes,
I stagger blindly,
seeking a path I cannot find.
And all I want is a bit of rest and a little rain.
That the dry sandy wilderness would agree
to yield me back my life again,
even if only in a burst of transient life
that must die as soon as the sun shines again.

Sometimes, all we need is for something to work today, just today, and give us enough hope and energy to invest in tomorrow. We believe that the existence of gigantic metropolises, the presence of humans in space, and the fact that twenty percent of the human race is living comfortably in socialist welfare states show how well the human race has improved its lot. We see such peace and tranquility as the eventual destination of all our societies.

But when, in the privacy of our rooms, we witness children dying of malnutrition or preventable diseases on television, we are rudely forced to acknowledge that the blissful experience of social wealth is still very rare. After one too many images, we are tempted to suspect that the other eighty percent are not working hard enough.

We are tempted to begin believing that they could do something if they were determined enough to change their societies and do away with such senseless tragedy.

We develop the sneaking suspicion that people who suffer repeated hunger are lazy, undisciplined, stupid, unmotivated, and uncreative. We suspect that those who suffer from constant war are savage, brutal, and primitive. We believe that they don't have what it takes to organize power sharing in a civilized manner, that they aren't driven enough to make successes out of their community, and that as a people they have failed to embrace the ideals that lead to progress. But we never say such things out loud unless it is to people who share our suspicions—we don't want to be politically incorrect.

And so we, rich or poor, at least in public, profess to believe—indeed, we must believe—that the transient will somehow soon become permanent for all.

We profess to believe that with enough work, life will be the same for all. And we spread the gospel that when all of us embrace a certain type of government, economy, or mindset, the wars that have plagued continents such as Africa will be a thing of the past.

We profess to believe that when we learn to share common values, our joys, pains, and anguishes will also be the same, and we will learn to live with each other and gather strength from our diverse economic and social experiences.

We profess to believe that when such a time comes, individuals will be powerful enough to stop rogue elements from starting senseless wars or killing women and children. We will have a democratic society, one less barbaric, and we will no longer hate each other or do cruel things to each other.

And like a visitor to the wilderness, we long for rain—just a bit of rain. We want to see the desert yield flowers. We are looking for just enough rain so that we can show proof of our richness and show that we are a species in bloom.

And so it is that in the arid wilderness of human experience, we have become fixated on one-week blossoms of progress nurtured by the desert rain, even though we know fully well they will die as soon as the sun starts to shine again. We want these temporary blooms because—with nothing else but the gritty sand of painful realities for miles and miles, not to mention the hunger, war, oppression, and repression—we can point to such blossoms and say, "Look, here is evidence of progress."

We want transient blooms of peace even though we know there will be a new war breaking out somewhere, soon. We want transient blooms of social refinement even though we know there will be a new spate of rapes and hundreds of children dying of malnutrition and preventable diseases, somewhere else in the world today.

We will go on pretending that there is progress: we must. If we don't, we will despair, and that is why those wilderness blooms born of desert rain are so important.

And so we have all become complicit in the rainbow making. We pretend that because someone in some metropolis in the west slept comfortably, ate well, and wrote a report showing that we have made certain steps forward, it will indeed be so.

And in the media somewhere, another important person marveled at some recent technological advancement. And what is the measure of success but the individual's experience? And if the individual's experience is the personal measure of success, then which individual is best placed to know we are succeeding than the one who has already arrived?

And so, from the far-flung valleys to the hills of this continent, we hear of echoes of rain, and we smell the fleeting fragrances from wilderness blooms.

The fog has broken today;
the blighting sun finally set.
The pounding rain has dripped to a halt.
The pummelling wind died out.
Today, hunger and famine is replaced by plenty,
plenty replaced by hunger and famine.
Laughter comes to an end,
sorrow lifts.
Today, yesterday's bitterness dissolves,
but the pain and bitterness of today will replace them.
Somewhere today, hatred grows cold,
and love warms up.
Somewhere else,
love grows cold,
and hatred warms up.
Everywhere, the children grow up
and learn all of our prejudices.
Old men begin to die,
and unlearn all they learned before.
New leaders have come and gone;
old policies have changed.
Yet the faces I see remain the same.
Yesterday we greeted the newborn among us,
today those we love will die.
Time has flown,
we have become old,
and finally,
we begin to understand the meaning of youth.
Today, nothing stays the same.
And yet nothing changes.
Today, life goes on.

I often feel very old—ancient. I feel as though I have been living in this world too long. I cannot shake the feeling that I have been here before, seen these faces, and listened to these voices—life is so familiar.

It seems I have walked this way before, that I have thought these thoughts, felt these feelings, laughed this laughter, and cried these tears many, many times before.

Much appears to change, yet at a deeper level, it is as if one community exchanges the dehumanizing experiences of war, poverty, and ignorance for progress, only to be replaced by another group, going through the same process.

Despite the appearance of progress in human affairs, we remain as heartless toward each other as we were when as a species we learned to walk upright.

We are still just as blind, ignorant, and unfeeling; unresponsive to the overwhelming despair of the majority as we might have been when our entire world, our reality, consisted of just a tiny cave.

We do not learn at all from our mistakes. We repeat them over and over, in different places, with different consequences—but repeat them we do.

I feel that I have been here so long, watching, listening, and wondering how long it eventually takes before we really learn. I cannot shake the feeling that life is so familiar, and I have been here before—many times before.

There is so much we don't say. And maybe even when we try to say it, we do not achieve our purpose. There is so much we cannot express, and maybe nobody is willing to listen.

There is so much that hurts us, that makes us happy, that makes us proud. But the laws and rules of our societies—what we can or cannot say and how we can or cannot say it—mean that the words are trapped long before they ever escape our mouths.

And I hope and long for a time when we will find another way of communicating, a time when you can feel what I feel, and I in turn can feel what you feel.

Then maybe I will know what it is like to be you, and you will know what it is like to be me. And you will feel my shame and my pride, and I will know what love means to you, and why you hate.

It is within our reach to do these things, but we are not yet willing. We are afraid of what we might discover if we really see, if we really hear. We fear that if we listen and really see, then we will find out something we don't want to know. Something that could prove that the things we think make our own community special and better than others actually don't. We suspect we might discover that the ideas we called foolish and impractical are actually better. And we fear that if we discovered we were wrong, then we would find ourselves adrift, with none of the familiar beliefs and platitudes to hold on to. Something at the back of our mind tells us that if we really listen and hear, then we are likely to find out that we are wrong about many things we hold dear.

We don't want that. And so we refuse to find a way, we refuse to hear, see, and share. We determinedly take this horrible logic to its tragic conclusion. We fight wars to silence difference and to silence the voice that threatens to change our way of life, the voice we fear will lead to chaos. We want things the way we are used to, the way we want them, and the way that serves us best. We want to do things to the way we have always done them.

We do not want to hear of alternatives that work just as well or better. We hurt, murder, and destroy rather than listen and change our perspective. We massacre rather than give up the ideals we believe are the best. We want others to accept our way as the only way. We will not let go, we will not listen: we would rather kill.

So we kill most of our modern prophets, those who would show us another way. For those who survive, we educate them and school them in our myriad of causes. We baptize them with the fire that burns in our various philosophies and beliefs, and now, firebrands they are, they carry the flame for us. They propagate and preach the fire that bakes us ever more solidly into our rigid positions. We need a new faith; we need a new way of life, a way that allows us to grow together rather than live off the ever-rising mound of those who do not see it our way.

We long to fly, to do things never done before, surpass everyone's expectations—defy gravity. We know we were born for much greater things and therefore we hope, plan, and aspire that one day, our species will transcend the vast expanses of space, travel to far off stars, see marvels.

The distances involved in achieving such a goal are so immense they defy comprehension, but we remain undaunted. We dream and we do. Space, we say, is our final frontier, the challenge we have to beat.

There is another distance similarly awesome and frightening in its immensity. If you have ever observed two minds, holding apparently opposing ideas, and unwilling to compromise, then you know of the vast distances we still have to cross to find each other; for the distance between two closed minds is so vast that no travel in the fastest of ships can possibly bridge it.

In our dreams, we believe our civilization will one day acquire the means to travel in a heartbeat to other worlds—other galaxies. We imagine exotic spaceships that would take us there. But to bridge the gap between one mind and another closed to it, how can that possibly be done?

I watch the lamp flame flicker
as its reserve of fuel ebbs out—
It is dark all around me,
but it shall soon be light.
It shall soon be light in my heart.

We tell ourselves a few lies to help us make it through the day…

The church stands upon the hill
like a sentinel
watching over us.
But it is of no reassurance to me—
It stands on the hilltop,
real,
unmovable.
Even from afar I can feel the stirring of the cold wind
that moves around its empty spaces;
I can feel the silent cries of those who have died there.
I hear their agony,
hear their pain,
smell their fear,
and feel their disbelief,
their shocked disbelief.
It shouldn't happen,
it can't possibly happen,
and yet it has.
Yet it has.

We live our lives based on assumptions about how things are supposed to be. We want to believe in a world that progressively gets better, where people learn from their mistakes, and the problems of today quickly disappear to be replaced by problems of tomorrow.

Yet life, by and large, changes little—and, yes, though we do find new ways of dealing with the tragedies and conflicts around us—the fact that they exist and the why of their existence changes very little.

Indeed, despite the layers of civilization and history, things remain the same whether you are looking in the Nazi death camps in Europe, the killing fields of Cambodia, or a tiny church littered with bones and skulls in Nyamata, Rwanda.

In each of these places, one finds the sheer unpredictability of human cruelty and kindness, the incredible lengths we are willing to go to kill or save, and the myriad distorted notions of what it means to be powerful, great—better.

For at the basis of each human cruelty we encounter this vicious and always murderous attempt by an individual or a group to assert its greatness over another. And in the amazing acts of kindness that take place, we see a fleeting recognition of fraternity.

From eternity, religious wars are fought on the premise that one belief is better than another. Genocides take place on the basis that one group is better than another. And all discrimination is premised on the fear and perceived necessity to stop "base and barbaric cultures" from besmirching the valor of our own.

Our bigotry lives off the fervor to protect our so-called "cultural purity" from encroachment by other cultures that would threaten the existence, uniqueness, and separateness of our own group.

And all the purges that have taken place are based on the idea that one group is better, holier, and healthier than the other, and its members must protect that state from encroachment or contamination by getting rid of the other group and its base, uncivilized, and dangerous influence.

Indeed, there seems nothing as common, even in our scriptures, as the idea of a chosen and a base group, a favored and unfavored group, a group supernaturally endowed with rights and privileges and another not endowed with them.

For what on earth does the Christian God mean when, in Romans 9:13, he says, "Jacob have I loved, but Esau have I hated." Long before the two are born?

And how can a group descended as it was from this "hated" group ever hope, ever dream, or ever aspire to win back favors so arbitrarily dispensed by the gods?

We have borrowed this thinking and imposed it on every arena of human life, in economics, religion, politics, and culture. And everywhere there is a group/individual/society saying "I am better than you and I have the right to rule over you, to preside over your existence, to civilize you, to democratize you, to educate you, to evangelize you, to make you as good as I am," or simply, "I have the right to conquer you."

And human beings engage in the most terrible of cruelties simply and for no other purpose but to show just how much better than the other person they are and why they, and not the other, deserve the riches of the earth.

You asked what I know about God,
there is little to tell.
He lives in the church,
and seldom leaves his rest
to intervene in the affairs of men.
God presides over the good.
He has no role in the bad,
and so I don't bother asking him
where my children are.
That question I ask the devil,
he is the one who knows where they lie,
those scattered gravesites that I cannot find.
No, I don't know more about God.
I have no reason to try.
He likes people with stainless lives,
and if I met him,
we would not get along.
It's not for lack of curiosity, or something like that, no.
I could think of a question or two I might like to ask him,
like why he is not content to live with angels
why he must make men,
let them frolic as they please,
and then issue punishments
to belatedly make things right.
I see your umbrage at what I have said.
See, I told you,
Him and me,
we wouldn't get along.
No, I don't love God much.
There I have said it,
now let me be.
I understand little of him;
I see no way to stop him.

They say he does these things to teach us lessons:
I see no lesson in allowing thousands of people to
die.
And if we must blame the demons,
shall we then say he is powerless to act?
Then how can he be God?
Enough then about such vaunted beings.
This world is made of men and worms,
creatures that stick to the ground,
except in a few famed moments of glory or flight.
Let's talk about things earthly,
earthly cures if you please.
Tell me about the hatred there is in men
and what put it there.
Give me visions of how we can un-put it,
and maybe you and I will finally be making some
adult steps.

I have problems with the Christian church. I must admit I didn't always.

When I was younger, I was nothing if not attached to the church, and with good reason.

I grew up feeling as if I was constantly in the middle of a whirlwind. With nothing else to hold on to, I clung rather steadfastly to the church. I adhered to the church's teachings, did everything possible to meet its demands of perfection, and constantly sought that acceptance which only the church seemed to be able to offer—the acceptance of man and God.

But there was always that Damocles sword hanging over my head, the threat of punishment if I failed to be holy, the possibility that I could die after committing some sin, some fault, and then all that I have struggled to achieve would be in vain. There was, at the back of my head, that niggling voice of doubt saying I was not good enough, not clean enough, and not holy enough.

There was a constant desolation that sprung from wanting so badly to attain this standard, this goal, yet all the while suspecting that I could not. Each time the doubts came, I would redouble my efforts to get God on my side. I would weep, fast, pray, and plead with God not to throw me by the wayside. In the church society, I was constantly shown examples and images of Christian uprightness to aspire to. I suspected I could not be as good as the role models, and the fact gnawed at me, gave me feverish nightmares at night, and filled me with feelings of guilt and dread. I worried and analyzed my actions daily, checking for everything that might anger my God.

I felt that if he let go of me, I would be nothing without him. I was so emotionally and physically destitute that I could not imagine living without the protection of this greater other, this powerful other. This greater other was the only thing that stood between me and utter physical and spiritual poverty.

Therefore I struggled to be perfect, watching every action lest I angered him enough to make him punish me, I could not see how I could survive such a blow if it came. In the end, I failed. I lost track. I despaired.

My love affair with the God of the Christian scriptures died as all other love affairs die. I found that my heavenly lover and I had inherent qualities that were mutually exclusive.

I could not negotiate with a being that lives only in absolutes. And how could a being that knows only holiness understand what it meant to be human, flawed, unable—sometimes unwilling—to be holy?

I wanted a God I could relate to, a God who understood what it was to be me, a God who understood what it meant to fail. I wanted a God interested not merely in picture-perfect Christians, but also interested in the rest of us mortals. I wanted a God interested in the woman taking flowers to the temple of Goddess Kali, the young man making daily prayers to Allah, the Indian holding rituals to the sun, and the man who had no reason to believe.

I wanted a God who suffers. Not once on a cross for a few hours, but daily—a God who feels the pain of rape and violence, a God who feels the pangs of hunger, and who can reach and heal a distorted mind that hates and kills.

I wanted a God I could be sure worked daily to change lives and redeem life from itself. I felt deeply that if a God cannot understand and cannot identify with life as it exists, if he is so holy and completely divorced from sickness, sin, and pain, then he cannot possibly heal them.

How can he act upon them?

The God of the Christian scriptures was supposed to be a loving God: his love was supposed to be represented by his willingness to let his son leave heaven and come to earth to die for man. It was said that he has gone back there to sit in judgment of us all. A God, here for a short time, to make a point of how holy he was, then leave to show us all how very few of us had made the standard. I began to feel very far apart from that God.

I began to realize that I could not hope to attain holiness no matter how I tried, and no matter how much heavenly help was supposed to be available. I felt trapped: doomed to perpetually try to reach this standard and fail. I was tired. I didn't want to try anymore. I wanted simply and only to be human.

My bitterness brought even more terrible questions. Why did this God have no hesitation in allowing thousands to be killed, raped, and mutilated? Is this the way they paid for their sins? And instead of consolation, he promised to send to an eternal hell of horrors all those who, despite their circumstances and anguish, failed to be good enough. I could not understand.

The Christian God came to represent to me a frightening reality. A powerful being one could not control, but who could do whatever he liked. A being full of vengeance, a being whose love I could not count on.

When my love affair with the church and its God ended, I felt completely bereft of safety and anchoring. A loneliness engendered by my difficult circumstances multiplied hundreds-fold. I felt exposed, at the mercy of the elements and with nobody, no power to shelter me. I was completely naked, vulnerable, lost.

In later years, I would come across churches in Rwanda strewn with bodies, families living with children of rape, and people trying to cope with the horror of the pain and violence they had experienced. Something in me collapsed. Something deep, internal, and fundamental simply collapsed.

I could not get an answer to a very basic question: what good, to what benefit, is it for a God to sit in a heaven and watch women being raped and mutilated, only to wait for the end days to judge the perpetrator while, the victim lived out the rest of her life with the nightmare always on her mind? Of what good, to what benefit was it to allow a child to be born from such an act of hatred? And where did God expect this woman to develop the strength to take care of such a child? If I were to go by scripture, this woman would be punished if she failed: she would be punished if she refused to have the child. I could not relate. I could not understand. I was hopelessly lost. I could not reconcile life with the demands of this God.

Today I am still a believer. But I believe in another type of God, more undefined, more vulnerable, less powerful, more caring, and less omnipotent. I believe in good and that while there are powerful forces in this universe that want to destroy, there are others that want to build.

To me, reality is not what some powerful God decides to do on a whim. Reality is that good fights with evil, battles are won, and battles are lost. My heart now holds steadfastly to the belief that there is a genuine power for good out there, a power that truly protects, truly cares, and truly suffers with all of us. I do not know its name, his name, or her name, but he or she is the God who brings good out of even the worst things, the God who makes it possible to go on in spite and despite everything.

We are often urged not to think too much, as if human beings have any other faculty by which they can apply themselves to problem solving or any other faculty by which they can begin to understand their environment.

And we are told not to think too much about the complex problems in life, for we cannot solve them all—as if there is any other way by which man can begin to understand what faces him.

Upon reflection, one might at least come to an understanding of some issues even if not all of them. Upon reflection, one might become conscious of complexity: how one issue feeds into the other, and why there is no such thing as something simple and straightforward in this universe.

It's the only faculty that differentiates us from animals, and yet we strongly discourage its use.

We will gladly accept beliefs which have no basis in anything that we can see, but not a reflection on those things that we can see and touch. If there is a religion worth advocating, then I advocate thoughtful consideration of life.

I am not advocating mulling over things in a circular and destructive way, but thinking,—really thinking—trying to understand, facing an issue while aware of your biases and preconceptions, and trying to see if you can see something different.

Of course, this does not guarantee answers, but thoughtful consideration might allow one to see patterns, see things that refuse to fit in patterns, and hopefully, lead one to be less inclined to believe one person or group has all the right answers.

Unfortunately, such an openness to challenge and to seeing things in a different way is not something that is immediately rewarding. It does not necessarily make someone happier.

On the contrary, the more you understand about the world, its people, and the actions of which humans are capable, then the more vulnerable you are to pain, because it becomes increasingly difficult for you to distance yourself from the fate of those around you. Maybe it is in an effort to flee from this painful identification with others that we are urged so often not to think too much about problems we are assured we cannot solve.

But there is a payoff in reflection, for even as you are forced to confront the darker side of humanity, you also start to see the extraordinariness of life, the great number of people who are inherently good, the courage of every day living, and the potential we so easily ignore.

You also begin to see angels, unsung and unheard heroes, who have reflected on life, and the reflection has led them to act, to soothe the pain of others, meet their needs, and heal their wounds, even with no one around to make plaques and statues in their honor.

You begin to understand that, as human beings, we are capable of so much more, if only…

Such a faith requires no temples, no rites, no masses, and no organized prayers.

Its teaching comes from life, from observing, reflecting, learning, accommodating, and growing. It is true that deep reflections on life tend to create overly withdrawn, anemic souls, trying as they are to make sense of a world that has so much senseless anger, hatred, and violence. Life is indeed easiest when you do not think too much about it, and those who choose otherwise choose a difficult path.

It is true that a deep reflection on life can break you. But it is as though out of such brokenness that you really begin to see. And when you do, you bloom; suddenly, you are full of wonder at the immense potential of humanity.

Reflection without action is meaningless philosophizing. Those who truly reflect become driven by the conclusion to which they slowly arrive: that the true tragedy of humanity, far beyond what we do to each other, is that amount of potential we waste.

It is a discovery that changes your life completely, because once you see, truly see, then you know how unsustainable our current way of living really is, that inevitably there will come a time when humanity will be called to reckon.

One day, humanity must make a choice to grow or die, for we cannot continue to waste lives and the talents that they bring with them in the way that we do now. What we can hope for is that we will learn not to be afraid. That, when the time comes, there will be enough real awareness to drive us to make the right decisions. That, when the time comes, we will no longer be like children and will take responsibility; become an adult species able to recognize how intricately bound together the fates of each individual are and why it is impossible to achieve anything while leaving others behind, or at the cost of their freedom or their well-being.

The hills are dusty;
not a blade of grass in sight.
It is long since it rained.
The earth is parched
spread out like the dried out hide of a long dead cow.
Pools of water are all that remain of mighty rivers.
The black clay soils
have turned into a thin sooty film,
gray dust covers everything.
Herders look out into the distance,
hoping for a cloud on the horizon
any sign of relief—
None comes.
The earth has given up on us:
the skies are clear,
there is no rain,
no promises of any to come soon.
The trees have shed their bark,
they are smooth as though oiled.
Green sap sinks ever deeper,
a tenuous wetness deep inside,
but outside, it is over—
Life out here has died.
Only the dust blows,
choking any greenery that remains,
and it tires the eyes to look at the famished plains.
The world around us is dying,
and we too,
and we too.

We need refreshing. Long, dry days may breed resilience, but to thrive there must be water.

Once upon a time, the folk stories say, there were men and women who could call down the rain, bring refreshing newness of life. And so when I weary of the hunger and thirst around me, when I despair for solutions for the parched land that is my continent, I dream about rainmakers; I dream of us rediscovering the power to refresh, succor, and bring newness of life to this, our dying land. But it is an impossible dream.

Rainmakers come from a different order of belief, one we had before and no longer have.

We have become something else, a hybrid between African and Western cultures, and the mythology of our new faith speaks not of rainmakers, but believers having springs of living water that bubble up to everlasting life.

The rainmaker was responsible for the nurture of all—man, plant, and animal life. But our new faith is a faith of each individual man. And the springs of water our new faith promised have become clogged up with rules and expectations. The waters have been tainted by bitterness, violence, and poverty.

The springs have stopped. Ease, ignorance, and arrogance have left the individual without the time, energy, or the willingness to let the spring water bubble forth, touch and heal the earth, its animals and all. And so I have been dreaming, wondering if our ancient gods, now that we have forgotten them so long, would deign to give us this knowledge again.

I wonder if the shrines we have forgotten for so long can be found again, wondering if anyone retains the knowledge required to make us rainmakers, a people able to redeem their land from the ever-spreading cancer of death and destruction.

I dream of a rain that would come not in a deluge, but a gentle shower, and of rain water that would cleanse away the confusion of identity that pervades our lives, bringing a new season, a new belief in ourselves, a new creativity, a willingness to work, make it change, renew this land.

And I imagine a time when the drought would end, and we would rediscover beliefs that encompassed all that is good, beautiful, and different, beliefs that can nurture the unique and different ideas, make them grow, and become part of an emerging reality of self and other-hood.

And I wish for a time when children would grow up stable, nurtured by a faith that values not fixed knowledge, but growth and discovery, bringing newness to every activity, creating the possibility and opportunity for people and things to grow, thrive.

Thus, my troubled mind dreams of a time when we will make things work again. And I will no longer fear the dark; I will not fear what I might find there, for there will be no more nightmares of war and violence. There will be just good days, rainmaking days.

She was a tiny girl
in a white and blue dress,
trying hard to please impress,
failing.
She wanted them to know she had made it:
she had gone to college
met a man.
But they saw only what she did not want them to
see:
the gawky,
awkward girl they had known.
And that she had loved a woman.
That she had loved a woman,
that's all they wanted to see.
And her white and blue dress,
the college degree,
and her impressive job
didn't make any difference.
She was still a failure.
Women don't love women.
That's the way it is.

Life seems to require so much of us,
forcing us into a constant letting go,
requiring of us a never-ending rationalization of life,
just to help us bear up.
We let go of the comfort of being young and naive:
we let go of the freshness of youth and not knowing
better.
We let go of beliefs we had about relationships
and how they work,
we let go of the unflagging belief that all humans are
good.
We let go of our dreams of omnipotence,
we let go,
we let go,
and finally, we let go of life,
and we die.
In the meantime, we preach false sermons
to our children,
and tell everyone who can listen—
anyone who needs an answer—
that it is okay,
that things are not so bad,
that others face much more difficult trials,
that it is God's will—
He has something special planned for them,
and all he wants is to prove our trust in him.
When that doesn't work,
when the promises fail to correspond with reality,
when our beliefs
in our holy God
fail us,
then we create scapegoats.
The devil.

The politicians.
Poor planning.
Lack of faith.
We scramble through the darkness,
trying hard to explain it all,
trying to explain the why of human tragedy,
trying to explain to ourselves
why there is so much misery and pain.
We grab at
anything,
anything at all,
any reason that will bring some semblance of order
in what is a truly frightening reality
that tragedy and pain don't make sense.
That there is little or no explanation for war and
violence.
We don't understand.
We really don't understand.
So we tell ourselves a few lies,
to help ourselves make it through the day.

We never talked about it.
We did everything we could to hide from it:
laughed a lot, cried alone underneath the bed sheets.
We cried quietly;
soft whimpering noises, afraid to be heard.
Private tears.
Public smiles.
And what awful games we played with each other.
Pretending to listen.
Pretending to be there.
And how we hurt each other.
It seems such a long time ago.
And I cannot understand now why we were so afraid,
why we had to be so alone,
crying away our loneliness and pain in the privacy of darkness,
keeping the whimpers down
so that nobody would know.
Do you remember?
Do you remember the time you saw me?
Do you remember holding my hand?
Do you remember the longing?
The need to belong?
How I wish we could live those days again
now that I have ceased to be afraid.

I could not and would not talk about her—for she was, and remains, a broken and wounded spirit, and it hurts me that it had to be so.

This unfortunately, is not an ideal world; it is not the world I want to be in, the world I wish I were in. If it was, she would have found help; she would have found acceptance. But she didn't. She lived a lonely, isolated life, trapped inside the wrong body, unable to accept herself as she was, and others unable to accept her as she wanted to be.

But nobody really talked about it, at least, nobody said anything helpful. Oh, they made jokes and made up stories. It is amazing how much wickedness people can ascribe to someone if they fail to live up to the image of what is "normal." What she was, in reality, was a lonely, wounded, struggling person.

She is lost now. I no longer know how or where to find her, and I don't know how I can communicate to her my continuing concern. I wonder why we had to be so lonely. I wonder why we had to hurt each other so badly. I wonder what she is doing now, wherever she is. And I wonder how long it will take before we learn to be kinder, more accepting, and more open. I wonder how long before we stop recruiting God into our campaigns of hatred and bigotry.

How long before we stop using religion to say who has the right to be happy and who shall be hounded and terrorized?

I am not afraid anymore. Like her, I found myself a child overwhelmed by many things I couldn't change, and I now understand the helplessness she expressed. I have also come to understand that it is okay not to be everything that people want us to be. It is okay to be just you, just what you are. I have realized that it's okay to be what I am. I sought acceptance long ago, and I did not find it. And in a sad way, it was good that I didn't.

It forced me to find the acceptance I needed within myself, and within a wider understanding of what God is and what we are. It also opened my eyes: I came to realize that as a species we are not yet ready to accept many things. It is the sad thing about us.

You used to see her ghost everywhere:
every time you locked yourself in the bathroom
or dimmed the paraffin lamp.
And yet,
you would keep her photo with you,
never letting go of it:
holding on to the memories,
keeping her near
though she haunted your every waking moment.
We have become familiar with our wounds,
and they have become like old friends.
Even the faces that haunt us
acquire a certain familiarity
and lose some of their menace.

The photograph was a treasured possession. I was honored to be brought into her secret. Years later, I still cannot define our relationship. I think she saw in me the child she lost, and I think I saw in her a mother, a caring person in need of someone to care for.

Like all relationships, time came and the umbilical cord had to be cut—a painful traumatizing experience. And we never recovered; we never spoke about it again. Time has made us drift in different directions, she a mother, me a single writer still unable to settle down, still unable to find a place to fit in. But I remember she used to see ghosts everywhere, and she loved to be outside when the moon was full and orange.

On the musty shelves,
I find books
calling me back to another day, another time.
I walk around
willing the days to flee,
to run away,
leave me free to breathe.
I go to the church
seeking the comfort of prayer,
and there is the silence of condemnation there.
And as I walk back,
children throw pebbles at the small of my back.
I sit on a grassy knoll
peering into the distance,
thinking of you
wondering what you are doing.
I try to reach you,
feel you.
I bought you flowers today,
I'm not sure if you will like them.
You are so far away—
I wish I could ask you
what color you would have liked.
I wish you would be here
shelter your head in my arms.
I wish I could hear your breathing in the night.
But I cannot,
and so I bought you flowers.

I think it would have been a boy. I don't know why I do; I just feel that it would have been a boy. But I will never know; I have thought about it often. I have often found myself weeping bitter tears about it. I have always wondered what life would be like if I had found the courage to have him, hold him, care for him. And I always wonder what he thinks now, wherever he is. I always wonder, but I will never know.

They found her body today,
cold
wrapped
in a flimsy sheet,
left by the roadside.
She looked as she had hours before,
when life still coursed through her veins—innocent.
They could not find her mother;
who knows what came over her?
But these are difficult days,
nobody hates her too much.
So they hurried to remove the body
it was a sore,
a reminder of all we have been through,
of all the things that have ceased to matter,
and of life that has slipped through our grasp.

It was a tiny church.
And there,
pious, young,
and innocent,
we spent our days.
There we fell in love,
married,
died,
received Christian burials…
We had full, complete lives.
What has happened?
What has eaten the old days?
Where is that place of comfort,
that place of belonging?
Why am I left wandering?
Why am I left searching?
When did we grow up?
How can I become a child again?
For I do need that comfort now,
that reassurance,
that belonging.
I do need that old simple faith.

I have missed the church. Not a day passes that I do not miss the ritual, the safety, and the warmth of thinking that I am one of the blessed few and knowing that there is that other taking care of me.

Each time the emotion overwhelms me, I go back to familiar churches, but there I find the things that chased me away in the first place: platitudes, easy statements, and a holy arrogance. I immediately go back to my loneliness.

Occasionally, I go to the church when there is no one. I sit and think, ask God many questions. Sometimes someone else comes in, and finding I am the only one there, decides to ignore my presence, prostrate themselves, and cry their hearts out—pray.

On such days I am filled with awe at the power of need, the power of desperation, and the humility of deep faith expressed by these people seeking out their God in the lonely hour, not when everyone can see their great faith and know of their great works.

At such times, I feel the church to be a holy place, a place set apart, where you can go and ask questions of an eternal being, an "other," an "all knowing" other. Sometimes I rail, and sometimes I leave there feeling more enlightened, as if maybe in that very private session of question-asking and sitting, that I am more aware of myself, and which way forward I should take. Sometimes I leave such a place all cried out, serene and tranquil, sure, beyond any reasonable and unreasonable doubt, that I am squarely on the right road, even if I can't see where it leads, even if I do not know which God has answered my cry for answers. It is in such moments that I begin to understand, at a certain level of my mind, that there is a reason behind being, a reason why we are alive. That awareness pushes me to discover myself, discover more—open my eyes a little wider.

It's a force that demands of me to ask hard questions, even if there are no answers, and to suffer the discomfort of having no answers rather than live in the easy comfort of a faith that consigns the bulk of the world to damnation, labeling them the unbelievers, the uncivilized, the heathen that we must convert— save—so that they can become like us.

I saw you today
as if for the first time ever.
I heard
when you whispered in my ear.
I look into your eyes
and see the fear there;
I see the wonder.
I see you today
as if for the first time ever.
I feel your warmth envelop me;
I sigh,
look into your eyes,
and see my emotions reflected there.
I see that you see me
as I see you now
like it was for the very first time ever,
and you hear me.
You see your emotions
reflected in my eyes.

THE RAMBLINGS OF A
TROUBLED MIND...

You lay trapped,
stillborn thought in the womb of my mind,
struggling to be born,
but stuck, half born, half unborn
like one of Michelangelo's unfinished sculptures.
You nag me all day and night
like an unhappy woman
that refuses to let go of a dead argument,
or like a tick
sucking at my energy and refusing to drop off.
So you are
a thought sharp and bewildering in its iridescence,
refusing to be put to rest,
refusing to be shushed
like a child, awake in the dead of night.
And all he wants to do is to laugh and play
heedless of his parents need to sleep.
And there you are,
the thought that will not go away
no matter how many tricks I try.
You are the thought that brings images through my
mind,
a whirl of psychedelic colors
heightened sense of smell.
I sprint away madly
to avoid listening to laughters that are never
finished
and cries that barely begin
whirlwind of emotions.
I have netted for myself a whale of
incongruous masses of thinkings,
and I wonder if I can ever sort them,
get a grasp of them, and force them to remain still,

at least long enough for a dissection—
vivisection.
For I must understand.
This is my endless madness,
this search for meaning that never ends.
And boy, what do we do
if we find nothing at the end?

I often find myself overwhelmed by too much thinking. Thoughts come and
never resolve themselves. Questions, relentless questions, and the only relief at
the end of it all is to write, to try and express, as if in expressing one can stop the
rush of ideas, questions, and thoughts...

The twin grave lies
amid the rotting maize plants.
The house is broken down;
the windows are cracked
there are cobwebs everywhere.
The headstone is unmarked.
cracks all over the cement burial site.
I wonder who they are,
the two people buried here.
There is no one to tell me.
The house stands
mute,
broken,
windows cracked—
Cobwebs everywhere.
And amid the rotting maize plants,
a silent twin grave
stands.

You stagger.
Drunk.
Incoherent.
Spewing vitriol.
Words that cut my heart like shards of broken glass.
And everyone stops to listen.
They take it for sport—
These words you scream
in your uncontrolled ire.
There is nothing left for me here.
And the memory of your face,
all twisted and screwed up by drink and hatred,
I do not want to carry with me.
Neither do I want to carry these words you utter.

There are events and emotions that refuse to put themselves on paper. They refuse because they create embarrassment, not just for the teller but also for those who are told about. Those events and emotions refuse to put themselves on paper because they are, years after they occurred, still fraught with violent emotions.

Writing is not easy: many times you really cannot say what you want to say. But I guess that often reflects life, because how often do we really get to say exactly what we wanted to say? So after writing, rewriting, and deleting only to write again, I end up with something that doesn't really say what I want to say.

A small girl
dressed in bright red school uniform,
sitting on the side of the road
in the dead of night,
weeps her heart out.
A house,
all lights on,
dancing,
music, alcohol.
A man,
drunk.
Telling the world everything there is to say
about her secret.
Feelings of shame,
embarrassment,
exposure.
Memories of a dark sky,
stars,
memories of humiliation,
wanting to run away, unable.
And so she sits, a tiny girl
on an asphalt driveway,
wishing to die,
but unable to take her life.
Longing for cover,

longing for protection,
feeling the desolation of knowing there is none.
Exposure,
a whole world of relatives to see—
Laugh.
Anguish does not register
because lights are on.
music,
dancing,
alcohol:
today is a happy day.

   I can delete it and write it again and again, but I can't capture the heartbreak, the shame, and the confusion. I can't make you understand what I see inside my head.

There is so much I want to say,
but words no longer say what I want to say.
They seem to have a mind of their own,
saying things I do not want to say,
meaning things I do not want them to mean.
When I look at you,
I know you feel me
and you feel what I feel.
You know what I want to say.
Let's dispense of words then.
They trip us up,
confuse issues,
and obscure the things we both know so well—
They do not express our emotions.
When I say love, what does that really mean?
How can it express what I want it to say?
When I say hatred,
how can anyone understand?
When I say fear,
how many know that wrenching, paralyzing emotion
that opens the bladder of a grown man?
I want to say so much,
but the things I want to say refuse to be said.
I try,
I force the words,
but they end up disjointed and all over the place,
they still do not say what I want to say.
Let us throw them away.
Feel me:
feel what I feel.
It will be enough.
You will understand.

I walk through life troubled. Well-meaning fellows advise that I take life less seriously: laugh more, play more. Loosen up.

The truth is that I cannot. Everywhere I go the stories I hear add to the voices already in my head. I try to forget the details, but I can still feel the person radiating pain, loss, confusion. Their emotions continue to wash over me long after the fact.

The rural areas that I visit are filled with terrible realities. The emotions of loss and defeat hang in the air like a sulking cloud that won't go away. Then I travel out of these tiny villages, and elsewhere life seems to go on heedlessly as if this other world doesn't exist.

Sometimes I think maybe I am not in on the secret formula that everyone uses to make these images go away, because for me they remain fixed on my mind no matter how I try to dispense of them.

And I see its impact on how I write. My writing is full of this gloom, and yet I feel I have to put it down or I will go insane. And so I think, I ponder, and I write: a troubled mind, a troubled soul.

A wisp of smoke,
some intangible madness.
A thought
I try to reach out and you elude me,
leave me pensive,
asking my many whys.
And when I rest, I finally find you.
And when I do,
I am lost—
What is this that I sought?
The knowledge has left me maddened,
unable to flee.
And yet
I cannot stay.
I dare not stay.
I cannot share,
for I don't belong.
I am not part of this troubling, maddening angst.
This tangled web of other-consciousness
constantly tearing at my innards—
I hurt.
And I wish I had not sought to know the answers.

The rain falls.
Pitiless drops
on the damp soil of my heart—
The cold stings my skin,
there is a musty smell of wet wood
smoldering at the hearth,
and ants stream into the house,
running away from the dripping wetness outside.
I long for warmth.
Instead,
the feelings of those around me
wash over me like a cold, gigantic wave,
drowning every sense of self.
I know not which to take to heart,
the hatred, the love, the despair,
or just the senselessness of it all—
Like them, I cry out,
hoping to be heard,
reaching out to you,
longing to be part of you,
longing to be held, and loved, and accepted—
to belong.
It does not come.
All that comes is the pitiless rain
and the cold that stings my skin.

The more I work in this region, the more I think about my life, about the lives of these people, and about life on this continent.

There is a certain sense of being lost here. It is both inside me and outside of me, as if my real self is out there and I have to find it to survive, as if our real identity is out there and we have to find it in order to survive.

I am troubled. So many things do not make sense. But I feel I have to get the answers somehow; otherwise, I might not be able to hold on to that thin thread that keeps me anchored to the world.

I live as if in an endless tropical winter where there is nothing but a ceaseless dripping rain of emotions: complex, jumbled, at once bringing relief, and at the same time drowning the self.

I have to find my way through the maze, through the mist, through the unceasing drops.

I search inside and outside myself. I search incessantly, trying to find meaning, trying to explain things to myself, trying to find a niche in which to belong, in which to assign these things I see around me, in which to carefully categorize anything so that there are no more terrible questions hanging out there without answers—but I am without success.

And finding that I cannot answer these questions, I ask myself why, and the process of searching begins all over again.

There were times
when there were cries of joyful children
stuffing their stomachs with wild fruit,
shouting in wild abandon—
A profusion of exultant sounds,
shrieks of delight.

The rain has eaten the laugher away.
It pounds relentlessly,
and the voices of cheer have been stilled.
The rain nourishes the earth,
but our souls have withered.
We have wept too long,
this endless rain
that falls from our faces.
Now there is emptiness—
Icy, cold silences
full of fear.

It rains suspicion,
anger—
Pain—

The rain has eaten the laughter away.

My earliest recollection of a rainy day is one April day, during a school break. I was eight. I woke up to a misty day, and the mist quickly turned into relentless rainstorm, which poured for most of the day.

Through the bedroom window, I remember peering at the bright orange April blooms being petered by the rainwater. I remember thinking about the unfairness of it all, that on a school break we were forced to remain indoors by this ugly gray rain.

My memories of that day are full of gloomy shadows, hazy, dark with fear, dark with insecurity, and loneliness.

Four years later, having been packed off to a small rural boarding school, rain developed another nuance. We had to run to and fro between the classes and the dormitories every morning and evening, four kilometers in all.

And for four months, from April to July, the heavy tropical rain came unfailingly. The heavy ceaseless drops were there in the morning as we ran to school and in the evening as we left school.

In those days, I rarely had shoes without holes. I can still remember the cold, clammy, uncomfortable feeling on my feet as rain water seeped in through the holes. And I recall the misery of having my white school uniform socks turning brown as the wetness from the muddy runoff seeped inside my shoes, found the white threads, and spitefully stained them.

Being rained on also evoked other deep-seated uncomfortable and illogical feelings; it stirred up an irrational need to stay in the rain, to be cleaned, purified, pardoned for a myriad of vague and amorphous wrongs I was sure I had committed to merit my hard life.

Tormented, I would sometimes seek out that experience; I would seek out that promise of cleansing the rain seemed to offer. I would stand in the rain, get soaked, washed through; in the vain hope that it would take away the feelings of being unwanted, the feelings of having failed to meet some unclear standard, and, most of all, from the defilement of acts perpetrated on my unwilling body.

I would pray, think, and hope for a cleansing that never came until much later in my life.

We ride in dark buses
on this, our journey home.
The weather is dull and rainy outside,
and the bus,
crowded and stuffy with the waste of life.
The sky outside weeps,
and so do we.
For we ride in dark buses
in the darkness of our pain
hurtling to our unwelcoming homes.
Homes we do not wish to visit,
but must.
And everywhere in the bus
the music cuts through our deafening silence,
reminding us
of what we must inevitably face.

I was told, growing up, that there were things you didn't say. That if something bad happened to you and you told someone about it, you were weak, spineless, and repulsive because of your lack of resolve to bear your individual burdens in silence.

Real strength, I learned, came from bearing problems without a sniff. Weakness was talking about pain, talking about loss, talking about anything wrong that had been done to you.

And so, though I longed desperately to speak out, I often didn't. And when I did, I picked the wrong people to tell—people who were in a hurry, people who were crossing my path at the instance when the silence had become too painful to bear, people only interested in the flesh, and what opportunity my need for company provided for them.

I made many mistakes seeking someone to confide in; someone who, I hoped, would not mind overmuch to sharing the growing burden of silence. I made mistakes that only reinforced my belief that talking about certain issues was not good, that talking exposed you, made you weak—fair game.

I am older now, I have learned better, and I should be able to do all the things I was taught not to do, but I find that I cannot.

Even to walk over in a cocktail party and make meaningless conversation defeats me: I want to retreat, run away—hide. And at the same time I want so much to be part of this world that careens past me, I want to be part of the world of fake smiles and easy conversations.

You see, we don't really need much from each other, just someone to be there to sit around with, and already all the burdens become easier. We think through them with more confidence because there is a human being seated nearby.

We trekked
day and night,
trying unsuccessfully to flee.

It was strange,
feeling the earth so alive and fresh in the April rain
and our souls so near death.

We passed by the abattoir;
how much like us they were!
The animals we once brought to this place for
slaughter,
but the abattoir for animals is silent:
men have turned to other killings.
The weapons that once brought meat to our tables
today cut down our brothers and sisters.
And so we flee,
hearts full of pensive memories.
Knowing that we live only in the now
none of us sure what will happen in the next step.
Yesterday is already full of dead bodies.
We have trudged for a lifetime
looking for the river.
There, we would wash ourselves.
And maybe—
Maybe part of the horror we wear on our souls
would wash off.
We have bent our faces against the wind and the
rain.
Heading to the river—
There we knew
we could wash,
and maybe some of the pain we wear on our souls
would go away.

Maybe some of the fear would wash off,
then we would face death with a lighter burden.

We walked for over ten miles. We were tired, but the older ones among us wanted to continue. Then we heard the sound of the river, clean water, rushing downstream. I have never been so glad to see water. We stopped, washed, and drank. It seemed the very act of resting that drained our last ounce of energy. We could do no more.

In my culture, dying is often referred to as crossing the river. Maybe it's just as well that we do not know what happens when we die: it allows us to imbue death with all the meanings that we prefer, whether Christian, Muslim, Buddhist, or animist.

We can think of it either as something to fear, or as a bridge to the perfected life. Or, maybe like me, you can hope that death brings a new life in another place, another time, and another form, and there you can hopefully see new things and learn new wisdoms.

Did you know?
They have introduced a new disinfectant
at the morgue.
I didn't know either.
But today,
sitting outside waiting to view his body,
I noticed it for the first time.
It stifles the smell of death,
sanitizes the place,
almost makes it seem clean.
I noticed
they have also planted new flowers,
and the new wing overlooks the valley and plain.
Sitting here, looking at the flowers,
I wondered why some bodies
are treated with so much respect
and others left to rot in the sun;
left uncovered on the pathways
for the dogs or the earth to destroy
at their own pace.
I thought about human beings,
why we have murdered for so long,
why we never stop.
How we can take so much pleasure
in the destruction of others?
Doesn't it speak of something
inherently twisted about us?
Why is the history of humanity
littered with dead bodies:
impaled, burned on stakes, stretched to their death,
dismembered with guillotines,
gassed in factory-like chambers,
or simply chopped up with axes and machetes?

And does it speak of any civil behavior
that we plant flowers
and take away the smell of death when, just a few
years back, we littered our streets with bodies?
Is there anything really human
about human beings except the name?
Where are all those high ideals we pretend to aim
for?
Where does this collective thirst for murder
come from?
How come we find it so easy
to justify killing each other?
Oh, they have come for me.
I have to go and identify my son.
They found his body in a drain,
too much alcohol—
Too many questions he couldn't answer.

They built a new morgue for the town when I was just about eleven. Even then, I was already an introverted child given to going off for walks to "think about life."

I discovered the new morgue on one of those occasions when my walk led toward the general direction of the hospital and its adjoining old mortuary. I didn't actually intend to go up to the building because, like all children, I had a healthy fear of the dead. I intended to go up to the edge of the compound and walk back. It was a trail with many trees, quiet, and there were few people.

When I reached the hospital compound, I realized there was a new building, and I was too curious to leave it unexplored. It was slightly set apart from the other hospital buildings, and early on a Sunday morning, there were no people around.

The back wall of the new morgue overlooked a valley. Standing there, one could see greenery and farmland for miles and miles. It was a quiet, restful place, and with no real understanding of the horror of death that it represented, it became one of my favorite hiding places. There I sat, for hours on end, wondering about my childlike world, asking questions of myself that I could not yet answer.

I have said goodbye,
walked away,
never again to return.
I have shaken hands with my friends, those that remain.
I bade them farewell.
It is over.
At night they will put me in a bus, take me
somewhere else.
I have no regrets.
This place has been a place of tears,
a place of great wounding,
a place of little laughter.
I have walked away from the bad
and the good as well,
all the things that went right.
I choose a place of no pain.
I start again.
It is not a rich life.
But who cares?
I am not looking for riches;
I am only looking for peace.
I cannot hold to both.
So am letting go of yesterday,
and I'm letting go of the pain,
even if I have to bury the good.

We have cherished many hopes
and even more dreams:
they have turned to dusty illusions,
and even the most demented among us
cannot hold on to them anymore.
They have torn not just our bodies,
but the fabric of our being.
How can we live anymore?
And yet we do—
That we do.
Wake up in the morning and face another day,
children laugh and try to play,
games punctuated with dark silences,
horrors seen that cannot be retold.
We live.
We smile,
share the same space and same wind.
We stare at each other often.
And we cannot see anything
but the dark abyss in each other's eyes—
You for taking my life away,
me for knowing that
but not being able to confront you—
Challenge you—
for fear,
fear of making it all come back again.
Fear of making the anger return.

I write compulsively, because I must, because if I do not express the things that trouble me, then I will be overwhelmed. I write the questions that come to mind, I write when I am in agony, I write when I am happy, I write when I am confused, and then I read what I have written and try to decipher what disturbs me, try and understand: I try and make sense of it all.

But words can be so unwieldy. I spend hours writing a piece, but it doesn't come out the way I want it to. I feel as if I have this ephemeral haze of words in my mind that frustratingly fizzle out before I can grasp a proper hold of them on paper.

And sometimes when moving from village to village doing my work, I feel these people share the same frustration that I have. Words to do not express any of the things they want to say. Words refuse to say what these people want the words to express—about their poverty, about their powerlessness, about their daily struggle, about war, about the wounds, about the deaths they have seen, and why they struggle to live, despite everything—or maybe even in spite of it all.

I see you rejoined with your children and wife.
Your life goes on.
There is a new shop in town
selling children's clothes.
The world is also moving on—
Those who died are being replaced by new lives.
And I remain here, like a lonely island.

Everything moves on, but I remain in the same place.
New cars,
new houses popping up everywhere.
Everybody rushing on to a new place.
I try to keep up with them,
but my heart hurts.
I know a place,
and that place was not far
when life was different.
But that time is now gone,
and I know we are building a new life.
We are trying to build a new identity,
push away all those things that went before—
Go on.
Move on.
Live.
I hear the whispers around me
wondering at my fixation.
Life is for the living,
not for those who are gone.
That's what they all say—
I will pretend.
What else can I say?
I can't speak,

can't say what is in my heart—
And I cannot describe the pain your smile causes me.

There have been two very significant men in my life—both of who are now dead.

One left me with excruciating memories that I have borne despondently until late in my adult years when their sting is finally waning.

He died tired, shattered, an emaciated man wasted by disease. I remember his question to me: "Can't you ever let go? Don't you realize life is moving on?"

Years after he died, I still couldn't let go. The pain has died out slowly and entirely by itself. I could do nothing to make its waning faster. Today when I remember him, it is with a different feeling in my mouth. I feel unhappy that I never confronted him, never challenged him, and never asked him all the bitter questions that stood poised on my tongue like angry wasps.

But I learned one thing from him: the perpetrator of a hurt tends to find it easier to move on than the victim. He is more eager for reconciliation; he calls attention to the passage of time to show the unreasonable nature of the continuing bitterness of the victim.

I have let go over time, but I wish I had found the courage to confront him when I had the opportunity.

The second man opened for me the possibility of a new life. He gave me a home away from home—a place to rest, a place to go anytime I needed help. In his circles, I found others who supported me; they held me up while I attempted to mend, to live, and find my way.

He died too soon: died before I had found my feet, before I had learned enough to understand life's complexities. I never fully appreciated his humanity. I did not attend the funeral. I had no money. I went much later.

Guilt-ridden, I was sorry that I had not been able to appreciate who he was when he still lived, sorry that I had not had an opportunity to know him better. I stood by his graveside, white flowers in hand, a priest by my side—one of many that had stood by me in those days—wondering how I could have been so blind, why we let the truly important people in our lives slip away before we have identified them and spent real time with them. I wanted to talk with him, but I could not.

And so I laid down some flowers on his grave and asked for forgiveness. I came back a year later, older, wishing even more than ever that I had talked to this man properly while he was still alive.

You came to ask for forgiveness,
but I had nothing for you but hatred.
Today I remember nothing of your face,
only your new, white sports shoes.
You were doing well.
I remember your pleading tone.
I think your mother had sent you
to heal the wound that you inflicted.
But my mother would hear none of it,
and I hated both of you:
you, for causing me the pain,
and her for not letting go and allowing me to live.
You are dead now.
More than 10 years dead.
And I wish I could listen to you now:
I wish I could hear your apology now.
I think it would ease my pain,
ease the wound.
I do not know if
it would change the way I feel about you,
but the fact that you are dead
makes it impossible to face you
now that I am finally ready.

I sit on a hill overlooking the low plains
and the meandering river in the distance.
The pain in my heart
will not go away.
The beauty that surrounds me
makes mockery of the emptiness inside—
People, like fleeting ghosts, come and go from my life.
And I am stuck in this moment:
stuck on the memory of your face,
the things that have happened between us,
and the pain I carry inside me.
I saw you in the hospital,
finished,
eaten away by disease,
And I did not know whether to be sad
or to rejoice
that there is some inevitable justice in this world.
But seeing you
laying there,
wasting away,
was still no satisfaction.

We were relatives and enemies. Bitterness and anger were the only emotions I had left—and he was dying. I resisted going to see him for the longest time; finally, I had to, for my own sanity's sake, and for my own peace of mind.

I little expected the emaciated man I found. Nor the doleful eyes of a wife and child. It made it hard to hate him, watching her, and that child. And I remember wondering to myself how a man who had caused me so much harm could be so finished, so defeated, and so small.

We made small conversation. He about how he had found God, found forgiveness, me about my anger, my bitterness. And I heard in less than a week that he was dead—we buried him. I cried for all the things we had done wrong, for all the pain, for all the shame, and for all the things in this world that never go the way we want them to. I cried because he was a waif—wasted, finished, lost. And he had gone and left his wife and child, fatherless, lost.

It is amazing how time changes perspective. Back in 1994 when he died, I struggled, trying to sort out the various threads of my identity that had become unfurled by the process of knowing him.

Time has passed; I have grown, and I have found ways of living with and dealing with the pain, the confusion, and the anguish of defilement.

And I understand now that, at the funeral, I had cried not to mourn him, but I had cried because of these things. Because, as hard as they are, we cannot undo them, we cannot unmake them, and we cannot unlive them.

Ours was a house of fear.
We let the stranger in;
gave him a bed with the children.
Now the house speaks of evil things,
and in the corners,
strange silences live.
And so sit we,
in dark corners of the blasphemed rooms,
shivering in fright,
willing the darkness to hide us,
willing it to be a dream
from which we will wake up...

I have to hope—nay, I have to believe—that the gods are not asleep, lest I give up and die. I have to find something that convinces me that the equation evens out in the end, even if I cannot see any hope of that, and even though there is evidence of decay, rot, and wasted lives constantly around me. I must dream, even if the dream is a nightmare.

I watched the sunrise today.
It was not pretty.

It was cold.
The house was closed to me:
I sat outside
through the pitch-dark,
waiting for sunrise.
And when it came, it was not pretty.
It was full of broken dreams.
Broken lives.
Broken spirits.
Broken bodies.
It was cold,
It was long,
and it was hard.
It was a terrifying daybreak.
I could see the light in the house,
but I was not allowed in.
And so I waited,
waited for sunrise.
And when it came
everyone went to his or her own business.
And the sharp rays of the sun
did nothing to warm our hearts;
did nothing to stop our shivering.
It is empty,
it is cold,
it is long,

it is hard.
It is terrifying,
this waiting for better things to come.

I have been waiting for the sun to rise, break forth in all its glory and dispel the gloom, the darkness, the pain, and sadness I have known and witnessed.

I have been waiting in this long darkness of the night for the sunrise, and everyone I talk to reassures me that daylight is just around the corner. Everyone that I talk to tells me that if I wait and watch, then it's not going to be long.

It is this waiting for sunrise that eats at the edges of my mind. Because with each hour that I spend in this darkness, I am expending precious hope and precious belief that things will get better.

And inevitably, the question has to come to mind "what if?"

"What if the better days never come?"

We sit, people waiting outside in the darkness, trying to catch some sleep in the cold air outside, frequently turning doorknobs, hoping that mercy will have prevailed. I have waited a lifetime—am still waiting. We are all still waiting.

The house is silent,
but in my mind I hear soft whispers
as if to echo what once lived here.
It is cold;
I cannot warm up this house.
There is darkness all around me,
nothing stays in its proper place.
All around are illusions and
whispers of warmth and comfort
that flee as soon as I try to embrace them.
I reach out,
grab at nothing.
Deep within my heart,
I feel the hollowed out parts.
I reach out and try to grab at something,
just so that I am not floating around in this empty
space they have left me in.
There is no sound,
no noise.
The house is cold and empty.
I can't find them;
I can't reach them…

Emptiness: I have often wondered why this particular emotion stands out so strongly, far above the feelings of depression, uncertainty, fear, humiliation, and shame that I have come to know throughout my life and my work.

Maybe it is the constant reaching out and trying to find certain relationships, reassurances, feelings of safety, but never finding them.

Children don't generally sit and worry: that is the job of someone else. So I associate emptiness with the arbitrariness of our childhood experiences, never quite being sure that we had any adult protection, being wary of what was going to happen next, and never being sure we could trust anyone to take care of us.

I associate emptiness with being forced to think about things children would not ordinarily think about, things that frighten you, yet you are not old enough to understand why.

When I was about eight, we bought a goat. He was rather a scary creature to me. I have never really figured out why we bought him. We were living in a quasi-rural area alright, but it was not as though my parents were particularly keen on that kind of agriculture.

The goat soon got sick and died. I was completely devastated: the thought that a living creature could die was simply staggering, and I was deeply shaken—I had learned about death.

A few weeks later, we came home from school and found that all the doors locked: no adults were around. I don't really know how long we waited; it must have been an hour or two at most, but it seemed like forever. And as day faded and night crept in, I can remember feeling forgotten, abandoned, and deeply afraid—I had learned to doubt.

I can point to that moment when I first felt unprotected and when I first thought I could not be sure that the adults would take care of me. I can point to the time when I first realized that living beings could die and the first time I was conscious of being forgotten or abandoned. But I cannot remember when I first felt empty.

It is as though it has always been there in the background, like a hole inside my heart: a deep, black gaping hole that refuses to go away. And now, even now, when, by all standards, life has become stable, sure, and relatively more certain, I find days in which I wake up, and, like a familiar unwelcome relative, it is there, lurking around my heart. Sometimes it hangs around for days like a gloomy cloud: not depression, not unhappiness, not anger or pain, just emptiness.

You have left me abandoned
on the side of the road
with no one to call to,
no one to help.
Bandits all around—
Where has the friendship gone?
My fate moves you not.
I see the features of your face
set as if in immobile stone.
There are no emotions there:
this is where our journey ends.
You have left me abandoned on the side of the road
with no one to call to,
no one to help.
Bandits all around me.
There is no remorse.
Let the gods bear witness to this bitter parting,
this avowed enmity that now exists,
binding us in an endless, needless circle of purging.

Dry leaves crunch underneath my feet.
The wind is dry.
The sun is high
gently beating on my uncovered forehead.
The smell of jasmine fills the air.
Jacaranda trees are full of purple blooms
which fall, littering the ground,
and go pop
every time I accidentally step on them.
The Nandi flame trees are in full flower.
Thin red needlelike spines are scattered all
around,
there is the aroma of life in full bloom.
The fruit trees are burgeoning with nature's largesse.
There are juicy guavas all around;
loquat trees drop their heavy harvest.
There is more than enough to spare,
and noisy birds chatter at the feast.
The atmosphere rings with
the sound of critters and small things
busily feeding, rejoicing in the abundance.
Animals are in gestation,
and noise of busy life abounds
in tweets, squeaks, squawks, and howls.

The only thing dead here is my heart.
The only thing dead is my heart.

The happiest years of my life were between ages six and ten. I lived in a school compound in a lush green, blooming rural town, with plenty of places and friends with whom to explore our world.

I often feel that my whole childhood comprised these short five years. That before and after that time, none of the circumstances of my life or that of my family allowed me any real childhood, any sitting back and enjoying life. Since then I have longed for the freedom, the ease, the joy of those days—and I have never quite achieved it.

There is a fog over life.
I cannot see.
I move like a man cutting through deep, dense
darkness to find light
(everything covered by deep impenetrable fog).
Light does not illuminate anything:
it bounces off the fog, creating
illusions of movement,
shades of light and darkness,
and as soon as a way appears,
it dissolves like a wisp of smoke
fizzling out of my mind
before I get my bearings.
I try,
I try to push through,
but then intellect bumps up on reality
and rebounds unsuccessfully.
I try to cut through the confusion,
but it is as if I cut with a blunt object.
I cannot fathom what is happening.
The more energy I put into the questions,
the more they come back to me,
like a ball bouncing against a wall
deforming its shape,
and as it comes back to me,
the question reforms itself
without any answer having been provided.
I cannot see the way forward.
I cannot see what will happen to us.

I remember once telling a kindly nun to whom I owe most of my present sanity that I felt almost as though I was two people in one. On the one hand, I felt as though I was a very old woman, tired and wearied by all that I had seen and gone through. On the other hand, I felt like a child trying without success to fathom what was happening to her world.

I remember that a heavy darkness, a feeling of perpetual heaviness, and an inability to see clearly accompanied life. I prayed a lot in those days—short, desperate prayers often broken by weeping and crying.

In that darkness, what I wanted most was a friend. I wanted someone who would not leave, who would not judge, who would not run away, someone with whom I could confide. I wanted, above all, someone to take away the memories and give me a new life with clear vision.

But more than anything, I wanted to be loved, held, and hugged.

I felt as though only a kind physical touch would validate me, that I was a ghostly figure and could only regain material form if someone touched me, held me, and validated my existence.

I ached. I was tormented by my inability to communicate this overwhelming need, which oscillated between a need for comfort and a need to protect my vulnerable self from any further pain and crisis. I wanted—but could not share—my private hell. Most of all, I feared the derision of those in whom I might attempt to confide: I feared that they might not be interested and that they might not want to hear me.

I was paralyzed by the realization that being acknowledged was not, after all, something that came automatically, that indeed you could, despite trying, not be of any particular importance to anyone. I did not want not to have someone interested in me.

And the thought that such isolation would be replicated through life overwhelmed me and filled me with panic. And it took many years before I could hold a thought in my mind without it being overwhelmed by shadows; darkness, and emotions that I could neither grasp nor define. I am still alone, but the darkness has become my friend, and, slowly, I have learned to see through it.

It is a familiar spot,
the vista permanently frozen in my mind.
Each incidence of pain
illuminated in all its various dimensions
of agony and grief.
It's time to say goodbye,
pack them all up,
put them somewhere on a disused shelf,
and move on—
lighter.
It is difficult,
but I have been here too long.
Longing.
Holding on.
Yearning.
Trying.
Praying.
Hurting,
and hurting others.
It must be kept away:
it is time to say goodbye.
It is sunset,
but there are still some minutes
before it becomes totally dark.
That is enough time for me to live,
really live.

One lady, when we were in school, accused me of constantly being in the process of sorting myself out, and she was right. I have spent many years trying to figure out what fits where, and why. I have tried to arrange the bits of pain and sorrow in perspective so that they do not overwhelm my every day life.

I am not an easygoing person. I am completely unable to just let things be and let live. And so I have spent hours poring over everything, trying to understand.

Finally there comes a time when one must eventually shelve these things. It is a few minutes before the darkness that must eventually descend on each of our lives as we move on to the hereafter. And I reckon now that that's enough time for me to live.

I nurture this new life,
gently,
like a flickering flame that must not go out.
I hold it
in awe,
like an egg with a fragile shell
that I must deliver home safely.
It is a hard won life,
the price paid dearly with pain, blood, and loss.
It is a fragile hope
and must not be exposed to the vagaries of the
world.
It is time.
We need to get a move on.
It is an unsure journey,
but it is the only way home.
And we must hold this new life within us
with all gentleness,
and fight with all our might to protect it,
because it is what makes us real now:
it is what defines us.

I have been on this road a long time. The questions I could answer have been answered, but many more will never be. And I understand now that the things we really are, the things that are truly precious, are fragile, vulnerable, and even ephemeral. I understand now that this is what we are: ephemeral creatures made solid, made real, for a set time, fleeting in and out of life.

For a few years, we are of solid state, and, for those few years, we attempt to play out our most cherished visions and make them permanent. Indeed, our brief period of solidity is characterized by this struggle, this reaching out, and this endless attempt at permanence.

Our years of solidity are filled with the pain of ages. We attempt, with varying degrees of failure and success, to overcome, conquer, and make what we are as individuals and groups encompass everything, override everything, and define everything.

And it is in this very blind and chauvinistic drive that we end up destroying so much, and then fleet away. And I hope for and believe in a time when we will awaken from our terrible dream, our nightmare, and see our very temporariness as that fragile thing that makes us real, and view our brief moment of solidity as a time to embrace, build, hold, love, give, and be.

And it is in this one thing that the writings we have built up in all our separate and diverse religions make sense. All religions speak of a necessary transition, a giving up of something in order to gain the other. A necessary initiation in which perspective is changed, and a realization comes upon us, revealing to us that the apparent is not the real. All religions seem to say that despite the things that would unmake us—even break us—life remains stubbornly alive, a tenacious grappler that refuses to let go despite its incredible fragility.

And this fragility of humanity is what must be allowed to unfurl itself, live, have its moment in the sun, so that it can take hold. For as a civilization, we have walked too long in the rain, we have toddled too long, fighting meaningless wars, unable to embrace the idea of humanity as a single organism—a time has come to awaken, mature, let go, and be.

Evening comes slow nowadays,
sun in the horizon a hazy reddish hue.
A soft lazy wind picks the leaves
and drops them a few meters off.
The neighbor's dog
makes its usual whining call for a meal,
and in the distance,
I hear the chatter of children
splashing and washing at the village spring.
Lately,
the air seems almost fresh
and everyone's smile, though tinged with
shared sorrow and bitterness,
is nevertheless warm and real.
I embrace the smells
of camphor and eucalyptus trees
and in the eye of my mind,
I see visions
of warm fire
warm beds,
and an evening that has been too long coming.
I put myself to sleep in peace,
and dream of my admonishment.
Open your tightfisted grip,
let go!
There is a rigor mortis over your soul!
Let nature breathe life
into your wounded parts.
Let the sun warm you,
the rains refresh you,
and let the greenery revive your hope!

Open your tightfisted grip on the past:
let go.

If there is such a thing as wisdom, then it is a rare fruit. If it exists, then it grows out of a gnarled tree, which gives flower rarely and in brief noncyclical and completely random bursts. If there is any healing, it must consist of real knowledge and real awareness of the rightness of time, events, and the necessity of deeds. It is when observing, as if from a distance, the very experiences that we are going through, that we finally know, understand, and then let go. It cannot be done any other way.

I wave goodbye to you with trepidation in my heart:
I know not if you will return to me,
and I know not what I will do, if you do not.
It is a rickety old bus that you take:
I know not if you will arrive,
and if it will bring you back safely to me.
But most of all,
I know not what time will do to us;
it might drag us apart,
you might meet happier days,
kinder faces,
gentler words,
and I might be relegated to old memories,
I fear.
I do not want to lose you.
I want to hold on to you forever.
I do not want to let go,
and yet I must.
I am not given an option,
so I pretend to be brave,
I hug and hold you,
then with trepidation, I wave goodbye,
not knowing if you will return to me.

Life has a lot of goodbyes. We are always saying goodbye to things whose time has come and has passed. Things we have believed and found to be false, goals we have made and achieved or which have now been overtaken by events, and ideas and beliefs held dearly and that we have come to find are not complete, not authoritative.

I am always saying goodbye. Especially to places I have been and have to leave, things I have seen there, done there, felt there, and I say goodbye to people, some of whom have been friends, some of whom have not been friends, and even some whose presence has caused great wounds. But this is one goodbye I have not said before.

It's a goodbye to old memories that have ceased to cause pain, and can now be safely consigned to the past. It is amazing how sad the process has proved to be, because pain and memories do become familiar, like annoying acquaintances whose presence may not always be welcome, but who are, nevertheless, a part of your life.

But there is something about a goodbye, because although it is like a form of dying, it is also, in a way, a promise of resurrection. We say goodbye when we have moved on to other things, other ways of doing things, and new beliefs. And today, as I die to some, I become alive to others: I grow. I become.

The sun sets to the west,
the bus rushes headlong toward the mountains—
I am coming home.
Wisps of clouds cover the mountaintops,
peaks jutting out above the clouds—
Bare, sharp, pointed.
Sparse grass dots the valley,
the bus rushes ahead heedlessly,
headed toward the mountain:
I am coming home.
Red-clothed Morans with their herds
are on the move.
Blue-clothed women with buckets balanced on their
heads take home foodstuffs.
This is pastoral land,
dry.
Sisal plants crane their tips toward the sky,
the grass is short and sparse over the bare, thin soil.
Thousands of cows
raise clouds of dust as they head home.
Giggling children wave us by
as we hurtle on toward the mountains:
I am coming home.

Putting these words down has been for me a type of homecoming. There have always been two parts to me, one terribly lost, lonely, and frightened by what I have seen and experienced, and the other trying frantically to make sense of it all. The lost one has finally come home to the other.

I am no longer in many disjointed pieces spread abroad, looking—but not finding—links with each other. I am finally complete, whole—at home with myself, at home with what I have lived through, and at home with what I have seen others live through.

There is a certain feeling of comfort and release when one thinks in terms of home, even when the actual home in which one has grown up is broken, dysfunctional, or nonexistent. I think this is the real success I have achieved in all my ponderings and writings—the separation between what can be explained and what cannot.

I have come to a place where you find the answers to the questions you have struggled with, but more importantly, a place where you finally accept that some questions will never have answers. It's a place where you come to the personal experience of being enough, and being able to embrace others—variant, oppositional, even unpleasant as they can be—because you are, and they are, and neither necessarily impinges upon the other.

That deep place within is a place in which you learn to weep for all the things that go wrong, the things you cannot change. It is a place where you learn to feel and touch.

It is a place where you become human, not just because you are a member of the species, but by sharing the reality of what being human means to so many others who are not you.

Home is belonging. Belonging to a reality greater than yourself, a reality that is constantly changing, a benign reality, a supportive one, one that heals us, in spite of ourselves.

And in finding this place, I can indeed say

I have found rest.
A Sabbath of the heart.
I understand now that love is not enough,
that people cannot fill the void inside.
I am at peace with pain,
and am no longer uncomfortable with joy.
Life, after all,

surprises us with either or both
when we least expect it.
I no longer struggle to prove myself,
to win love, affection, or admiration.
I know myself
and the ever-pressing need to learn more,
to let go, and then grow.
And in this one thing,
I have found a reason to live
and a reason to die.

I came across the phrase "a reason to live and a reason to die" in a Christian book about faith. Christianity, it was argued, tells us who we are, what we are, why we are here, where we are going, and why we are special.

Christianity, the book argued, answers all those questions by introducing us to a God who made us, is interested in us, and has died for our salvation. I have not necessarily accepted this argument. But I have made my peace with religion, faith, and the power that created us. A human being must have something to believe in; otherwise, they flounder. A human being must have something they aspire to; otherwise, they debase themselves. A human being must find meaning in life; otherwise, they become bitter, troubled, and empty.

I have come to believe that whoever and whatever made us could not have envisaged a uniform faith for all of us. How can the child born in an arid section of a war-torn country, who grows up to be illiterate, raped, pillaged, and then die of malnutrition by forty ever perceive faith in the same terms as a white boy, born in a middle class American or European home, with the comfort and luxury of engaging in a food fight?

How does having food in the refrigerator, summer holidays by the beach, parties in the teens, growing up to be the local sales clerk, marrying, and dying of a heart attack at the ripe age of sixty impact on your view of life, meaning, and purpose?

And so I must reject the notion that a being intelligent enough to create the universe would lack the discrimination to see that these two people can never have the same faith. Indeed, they cannot perceive God in the same way. More-over, they cannot perceive the universe they live in in the same terms.

And I have come to believe that there has to be a path for each of us, an expec-tation shaped by and delineated by one's particular gifts and possibilities, a god in one's own size, a faith based on one's own reality. Blasphemy? Maybe, but who knows?

I want to believe in a God who cares for each and every person, not just those with the means to understand. Not just those with the luxury of choice, not just those with the gift of a privileged birth. I want to believe in a God who empowers us to grow, to advance, to leave our childhood behind, and mature as a species so that we do not have to depend on the threat of his fury to get us to love and care for each other.

I want to believe in a religion that arises when our identities have matured and we can see in the face of each man the reflection of the many selves we might have been had we been born in a different place, a different time, and to a different set of circumstances.

The cloud has been gathering,
but I am not afraid:
I have been waiting for this rain eagerly.
I have been waiting for its cleansing,
watching for its washing
to clear out the dust that has been choking me,
this dust filling my gullet,
filling my stomach,
my nose,
and ears.
I have been hurting too long,
waiting for this rain to come,
waiting for it to fall.
My heart is parched—
blistered, dry.
It's been broken and is sore
waiting for this rain
that will bring life back into my inner being.
Would that it would fall on me,
would that it would drown me,
quench me,
sweep me away,
cleanse me.
Would that it would rain.

I began writing these pieces as far back as 1990. Over time, I have written, rewritten, destroyed, changed, and tried to hide what they really mean.

I would start and stop, rewrite the pieces again from scratch, try to reconstruct what I intended each to mean. But in recent years, I have had the feeling of coming out of the mist, finding my way, as though a heavy cloud is slowly and finally lifting away and a greater courage is taking root.

I still struggle to write; I still feel that some things go unexpressed despite all my efforts. But overall, I feel satisfied, content, and even relieved.

Today as I write this last piece, I sit in my tiny room facing the window, looking at the plant and bird life outside. I look at the plains, and from afar, I can see dark, stormy clouds gathering.

It will rain.

I have always loved the rain, and yet rain has always had other deep and disturbing emotional connotations for me, like suffering, cold, loss, and pain. And as I watch the sky preparing itself to weep, once again, words escape me. I find that I do not have the language to express what I feel at this very moment.

The smell of red volcanic soil is wafting into the house. A rich smell from the loamy soil, wafting up as if in anticipation of the water that must inevitably fall. Instinctively, I realize I have been waiting for this moment a very long time.

The day grows dark as the clouds roll in, fast covering the distant plains and the town. The rain starts to fall in thick, hard drops, and then heavily, with thunder and lightening. And for the first time in many years, I put down my pen, leave my room, and stand outside. It rains, the drops falling hard over my face, my head, and my whole body. I feel as though I am undergoing a very special kind of baptism, as if the heavens have deemed it right to give me a holy bath, to cleanse me, wash me.

I cry like a baby. It has been so long coming, this rain. It has been so long coming. And finally, I am free.

978-0-595-39653-5
0-595-39653-4

Printed in the United States
64754LVS00005B/369